THE FIRST REQUISITE

OF A GOOD CITIZEN

IN THIS REPUBLIC OF OURS

IS THAT HE SHALL BE

ABLE AND WILLING

TO PULL HIS WEIGHT.

Theodore Roosevelt

PICTORIAL ENCYCLOPEDIA

Volume 10
1901 to 1914
The Cry For Reform And Equality

of AMERICAN HISTORY

Dramatically pictured with new living art and stirring narrative in a series of authoritative volumes to enrich the interest and appreciation of young Americans in their heritage of freedom and equality

SPECIAL CONSULTANTS

Bernard S. Miller, ED.D.
Associate Director, John Hay Fellows Program; Collaborator with James B. Conant, *The American High School Today*.

Kenneth W. Lund, PH.D.
Superintendent Oak Park-River Forest High School, Oak Park, Illinois; Chairman, North Central Association Committee on Guidance and Counseling.

Kenneth L. Peters, M.S.
Superintendent of Schools, Beverly Hills Unified School District, Beverly Hills, California.

CONTRIBUTORS

Daniel Powell, M.A.
Teacher, Social Studies Dept., Senn High School, Chicago; John Hay Fellow, University of Chicago.

Commander William M. McCarthy
United States Naval Reserve; Formerly Officer in Charge Press Section Public Information, Navy Department, Washington, D.C.

Pearl J. Slaton, M.A.
Formerly Teacher Public Elementary Schools, McKinley High School, Chicago; Reader, Niles Township High School, Skokie, Illinois.

Earl Schenck Miers
HISTORICAL EXPERT AND AUTHOR.

Jerry Wolfert
HISTORIAN AND AUTHOR.

ILLUSTRATORS and GRAPHIC ARTS
Clarence Pontius • Arnie Kohn • Richard Potts • Charles R. McCurry • Lloyd Rognan • Robert Caples • Bill Law • William Gray • Francisco Torres • Steve Dobson • Russell G. Manning • Don Putman • Geraldine A. Simkus • Alexander Toth • Warren Tufts • Ray Vinella • Norman Dawn • Al Andersen • Bob Totten • Harry J. Blumenfeld • J. M. LaGrotta • Gloria Nehf • George Bures • Robert Boehmer • Jim Gindraux • Don Simmons • Helen Prickett

UNITED STATES HISTORY SOCIETY, INC.

Prestige And Responsibility

America stood head and shoulders in the front line of great world powers —conceding not an inch of stature nor a pound of weight to any nation.

A war with Spain had been fought to a swift and victorious conclusion.

The American flag floated in the breezes of two vast oceans with the acquisition of new territorial possessions in Puerto Rico, Hawaii, Guam and the Philippines. A protectorate was held in Cuba.

America's mighty new "steel navy" cruised in Atlantic, Pacific and Caribbean waters—a formidable guarantee of protection.

In the field of other foreign relations, the United States had entrenched its diplomatic influence without resort to force ... true test of a power's greatness. In world commerce, finance and desire for permanent peace, the nation had become a leader.

Now a truly great world power, the United States faced its widening future with confidence and full realization that it also had great responsibility—not only abroad, but very great responsibility at home.

"A splendid little war," Theodore Roosevelt called the clash with Spain. It lasted only a few months, but was completely decisive.

On February 15, 1898, the battleship Maine was destroyed by an underwater explosion in the harbor at Havana. The lives of 260 Americans were lost. Militant elements of the nation's press blamed Spain for planting a mine or bomb. The people demanded war and President William McKinley asked and obtained from Congress an ultimatum which forced Spain to declare war.

Two big naval victories, each of which smashed a Spanish fleet, and the land Battle of San Juan brought about the quick defeat of Spain.

Commodore George Dewey led a squadron of America's steel warships into Manila harbor and destroyed Spain's Philippine fleet on May 1.

On July 1, American troops charged up San Juan hill and routed the Spanish defending Santiago. Theodore Roosevelt led his famous Rough Riders in this battle.

On July 3, Admiral William T. Sampson's Atlantic squadron destroyed Admiral Pascual Cervera's Spanish naval force as it sought to escape from Santiago harbor.

With the surrender of Manila on August 14, 1898, the war with Spain ended. In the final peace treaty, Spain gave up its claim to Cuba and ceded

Puerto Rico and the Philippines to the United States. The same year, Hawaii was annexed.

America launched a campaign to broaden and strengthen its foreign relations. With the other great powers, the United States signed the Hague Convention which created the Permanent Court of International Arbitration. The Court's purpose was to settle by peaceable means the disputes between nations.

In 1899, Secretary of State John Hay proclaimed the Open Door policy in China, asking equal commercial rights for all nations. Also in 1899, the United States mediated a dispute between Venezuela and British Guiana. Hints of military action helped America's diplomacy bring Great Britain to terms.

Meanwhile, domestic problems confronted the successive administrations of Presidents James A. Garfield, Chester A. Arthur, Grover Cleveland, Benjamin Harrison, Grover Cleveland again, and William McKinley.

Labor's clamor for recognition of its rights rose ever louder. Many strikes resulted from disputes with management. Twenty-three were killed in the Haymarket Riots in Chicago and an anarchist-labor riot at Milwaukee.

Other violence accompanied strikes of steelworkers at Homestead, Pennsylvania, miners at Cripple Creek, Colorado, and Pullman Company workers in the Chicago area.

A bright ray of hope shone for the distressed workingman—The American Federation of Labor was organized in 1886 with Samuel Gompers as the President. Gompers and the A.F. of L. began a long career of leading labor to better working and living conditions.

In the field of business and industry, the development of trusts followed the lead of the Standard Oil monopoly. This was a major problem facing the government, the first move against which was passage of the Sherman Anti-Trust Act.

The "free silver" issue brought on bitter political controversy, finally leading to the nation's adoption of the gold standard. McKinley was elected President on the Republican's gold platform in 1896, defeating the Democrats' "free silver" leader, William Jennings Bryan. Again in 1900, McKinley defeated Bryan to win reelection.

As McKinley entered his second term, the nation was enjoying prosperity. America's position among world powers was established beyond question, but many chores remained to be performed at home.

© Copyright 1962-1968 by Davco Publishing Company, Chicago, Illinois, U.S.A. All rights reserved under Pan-American Copyright Convention and the International Copyright Convention. No part of the text or illustrations in this work may be used without formal permission from the publisher. Library of Congress Catalog Card Number 62-14937. PRINTED IN THE UNITED STATES OF AMERICA.

THE TWENTIETH CENTURY LAY AHEAD—

The nation's influence in world affairs was established. The Monroe Doctrine prevailed in Latin-American controversies. America led at international meetings.

America, now a dominant world power, faced the Twentieth Century with confidence — prepared to confront new problems and conquer them for new triumphs.

Big business made multi-million dollar fortunes. Industry became massive under big corporations. The federal government declared war on trusts.

Organized labor had many gains, but sought shorter hours and higher wages. The American Federation of Labor, under Samuel Gompers, had 2,000,000 members.

A NEW ERA OF STRUGGLE AND PROGRESS

Conservation of natural resources was regarded as necessary for the nation's welfare. Programs for forest, water, soil and mineral conservation were undertaken by the government.

Many wealthy Americans devoted fortunes to the betterment of mankind. Such philanthropists as Andrew Carnegie and J. D. Rockefeller endowed libraries and research.

Reform movements were intensified. Prohibition and women's suffrage were leading campaigns.

International tensions increased with the rise of major powers. Germany and Japan vied with Britain, France and Russia for supremacy. America became involved through its new global role.

1901

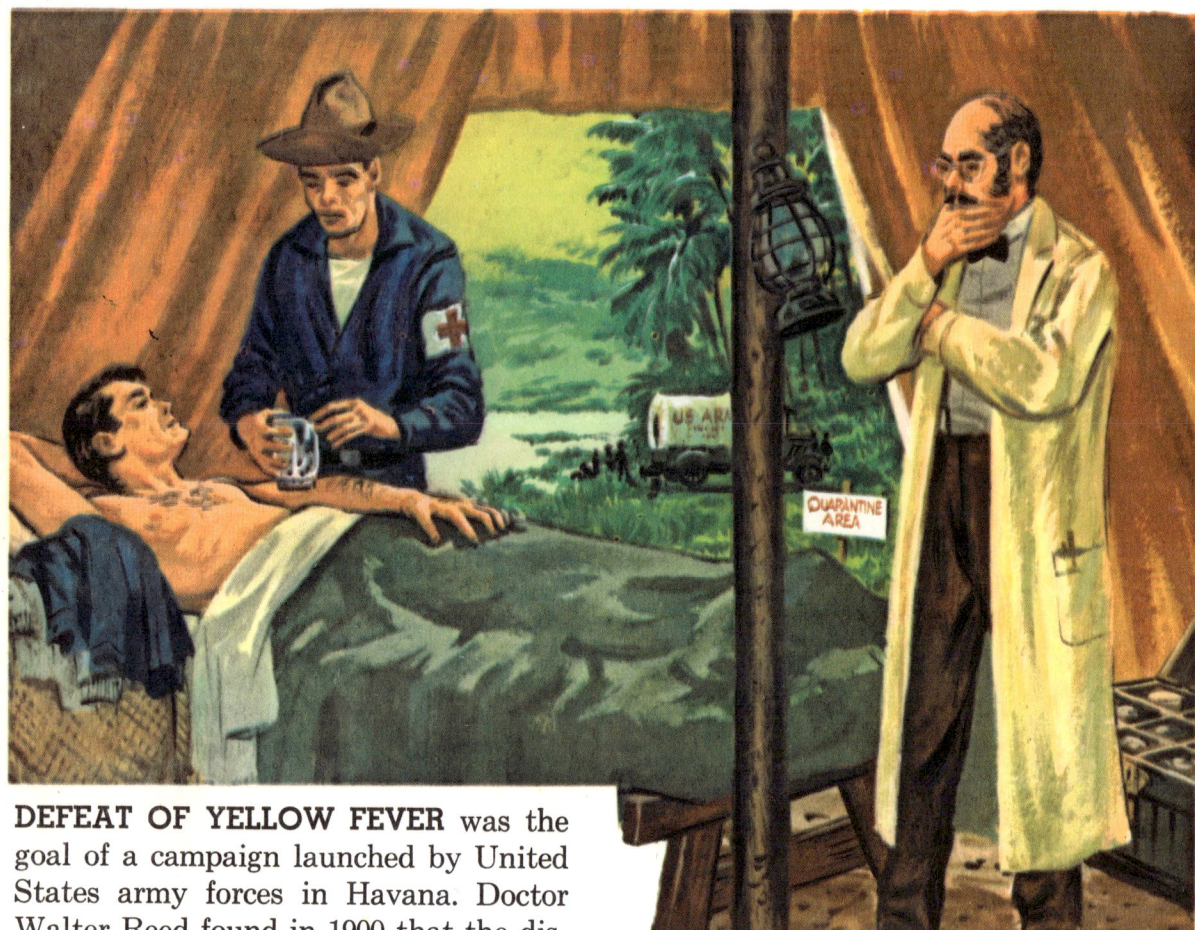

DEFEAT OF YELLOW FEVER was the goal of a campaign launched by United States army forces in Havana. Doctor Walter Reed found in 1900 that the disease was transmitted by the stegomyia mosquito. Tragic proof came when Doctor Jesse W. Lazear submitted to the bite of the mosquito, caught yellow fever and died. An epidemic of the disease had taken the lives of many American soldiers. Now that the carrier of yellow fever was identified, the army determined to control the disease by exterminating the cause. On February 4, 1901, Major William Crawford Gorgas began the campaign. Gorgas, the son of a Confederate soldier, was chief surgeon of American forces in Cuba. He had followed closely Doctor Reed's work in tracing yellow fever to the stegomyia mosquito. The Havana countryside was a natural breeding ground for mosquitoes. In the hot, wet and sticky climate, many stagnant pools formed. Gorgas had them drained and sprayed with chemicals. Swamplands also were drained for miles around. Underbrush and thickets were cleared and sprayed. All garbage was burned during the intensive drive.

In the course of the campaign breeding places of rats also were wiped out. Havana long had been infested by many tropical diseases, some of them carried by rats. By the end of 1901, Gorgas' campaign completely cleared Havana of yellow fever for the first time in nearly 150 years. Gorgas' methods were copied by other tropical countries and are still used in the prevention of yellow fever.

1901

CARRY NATION'S HATCHET broke many a bottle of whiskey on the counters of Kansas saloons. Mrs. Nation was a militant crusader for the prohibition movement, which gained impetus in the early 1900's. She carried a Bible under one arm and swung a hatchet with the other. Her specialty was marching at the head of a band of women prohibitionists into saloons or restaurants serving liquor. Using rocks and hatchets, the crusaders smashed bottles and wrecked tables. All places selling whiskey, whether legally or not, were considered by the raiders as fair targets. Mrs. Nation was arrested many times as the result of her raids. Her arrest on February 4, 1901, for smashing a saloon focused attention on prohibition in Kansas. Mrs. Nation had been married to a drunkard, Charles Gloyd. When efforts to reform her husband failed, she became an uncompromising prohibitionist. Following a second marriage, Mrs. Nation and her new husband moved to Medicine Lodge, Kansas. She formed a local unit of the Women's Christian Temperance Union and launched her stormy crusade against saloons.

The temperance movement had made much headway. The Anti-Saloon League, formed in 1895, obtained funds from donations and collections at churches. Forces of organizers were employed. The league urged heavy licenses for saloons, temperance education in schools, and total prohibition by law. The league pursued its campaign through sermons, speeches and anti-saloon journals.

1901

A POLICY FOR POSSESSIONS was placed in Congress' hands by a series of Supreme Court decisions in 1901. The major ruling, given in a group of Insular Cases, was that the "Constitution did not follow the flag." According to this decision, the annexation of a territory did not mean that the territory's residents automatically became entitled to all of the Constitution's privileges. They were not necessarily recognized as citizens of the United States. Constitutional rights and citizenship privileges had to be conferred specifically by Congress.

The Supreme Court thus gave Congress a free hand in determining United States policy for outlying possessions. The decisions upheld two territorial actions which Congress had taken in 1900. The Foraker Act set up a government for Puerto Rico under a governor and executive council appointed by the President, and a lower house elected by the Puerto Ricans. The islanders were declared to be citizens of Puerto Rico, but not of the United States. Hawaii became a territory with full constitutional rights.

The principle laid down by the Supreme Court differentiated between two kinds of possessions—those which eventually were to become states and those which would not. To the inhabitants of the former areas went all of the rights granted under the Constitution to United States citizens. To other possessions such as the Philippines, Puerto Rico and Samoa, which were not to become states, only certain rights would be guaranteed. But for all people living under the law of the United States the basic constitutional freedoms of life, liberty and also property were protected.

1901

SELF-RULE BY CUBA was authorized by the United States, with certain reservations. After the war with Spain, the island remained under American army administration, headed by General Leonard Wood. The Cubans were instructed to adopt a constitution for self-government. When drafted, the constitution contained no provisions for continued relations with the United States. On instructions from Secretary of War Elihu Root, General Wood informed the Cuban leaders that such provisions must be included. On that basis only would the United States withdraw military control.

Congress outlined the conditions for continued Cuban relations in the Platt Amendment to the island constitution. Cuba was to agree never to sign a treaty with a foreign power limiting its own independence. The public debt could not exceed an amount which normal revenue could pay. The United States would have the right to intervene in case of Cuban disorders or interference by a foreign power. Land would be sold or leased to the United States for naval or coaling bases. In effect, these conditions when written into Cuba's constitution would give the United States a semi-protectorate over the island. Cuba would not become a United States possession, but neither would it be independent. The amendments were added to Cuba's constitution on June 12, 1901, and the islanders began forming their government leading to withdrawal of American troops.

1901

PRESIDENT McKINLEY was assassinated while attending the Pan-American Exposition at Buffalo. He was shot by a crazed anarchist on September 6, 1901, and died eight days later. The President made a speech at the Exposition the day before he was shot. He hailed the end of American isolationism and the acquisition of island possessions. President McKinley discussed the state of America's commercial life and declared that reciprocity between nations should be the American policy in all trade agreements.

McKinley's speech was enthusiastically received. The next day he attended a public reception in one of the Exposition halls with a large crowd present. A man stepped forward and pointed his right hand at the President. The stranger fired two shots from a pistol concealed beneath a handkerchief draped over his hand. The assassin said not a word as he shot. McKinley fell mortally wounded.

The assassin was captured and identified as Leon Czolgosz, a young factory worker. Czolgosz, admittedly an anarchist, could give no reason for his act except that he hated government. He was tried and convicted in the supreme court of New York and was electrocuted in Auburn State Prison on October 29, 1901. William McKinley was the third President to die by an assassin's hand. Abraham Lincoln was shot in Ford's Theater in April, 1865, and James Garfield was fatally wounded in the Washington railroad station in July, 1881. Robert Todd Lincoln, oldest son of the Civil War President, was at the scene of all three assassinations. Lincoln had an appointment with McKinley and arrived at the hall immediately after the shooting.

THEODORE ROOSEVELT was given the oath as the twenty-sixth President a few hours after McKinley died. The Vice-President was sworn in as the chief executive at the home of a friend, Ansley Wilcox, in Buffalo. The oath was administered on the afternoon of September 14, 1901, by Judge John R. Hazel of the United States district court. Instead of a formal inaugural speech, Roosevelt simply stated that he pledged himself "to continue absolutely unbroken the policies of President McKinley."

Roosevelt was the youngest man to take the oath as President. He was forty-two years and ten months old. Roosevelt announced that he would retain McKinley's cabinet. Included were Secretary of State John Hay and Secretary of War Elihu Root. Hay had distinguished himself by his handling of difficult foreign relations. Root had assumed the army's administration of newly won territories. Another key member of the administration was William Howard Taft, who recently had been appointed governor-general of the Philippines. Taft was sent to install a system of government.

Theodore Roosevelt, well-educated member of a wealthy family, had an adventurous career. He spent much time on ranches in the Dakotas. He traveled in Europe and went on many hunting expeditions. With Leonard Wood, he organized the Rough Riders of Spanish-American War fame. After the war, Roosevelt was elected governor of New York. Previously, he had served in the New York legislature, on the Civil Service Commission, and as president of the New York police board. Republican conservatives considered Roosevelt to be impetuous.

1901

A CANAL ACROSS THE ISTHMUS of Central America was of increasing appeal to the United States. Several attempts by private interests to construct an isthmian waterway connecting the Atlantic and Pacific oceans had failed. The obvious value of such a shortcut in long ocean travel spurred America's desire to build and control a canal. In 1850, the United States and England signed the Clayton-Bulwer Treaty, guaranteeing that any isthmian canal would be jointly built and not fortified. By 1900, the United States no longer wanted joint control—but definitely wanted the canal.

The first attempt to build a Panama Canal was made in 1879 by a French company. After spending $260,000,000 on the project, the company failed and surrendered its franchise to a Panama Canal Company, formed to sell the French firm's assets to the United States. In 1893, an American concern called the Maritime Canal Company also went bankrupt attempting to construct a canal across Nicaragua. One obstacle in the way of the United States government undertaking a canal project was the Clayton-Bulwer Treaty of 1850. Secretary Hay conducted negotiations with England and succeeded in having the treaty abrogated.

A new agreement was signed on November 18, 1901. Called the Hay-Pauncefote Treaty, it gave the United States the right to construct and control, independently, an isthmian canal. Neutrality of the canal zone was to be guaranteed by the United States. Great Britain's only requirement was that the canal be "free and open to the vessels of commerce and of war of all nations—on terms of entire equality." A memorandum was attached to the treaty conceding the United States' right to fortify the canal. Only Congress' authority to build now was needed.

1902

ANDREW CARNEGIE, the steel multi-millionaire, gave most of his fortune to philanthropic causes. He established numerous trusts and foundations for research, education, world peace and other humanitarian purposes. In January, 1902, Carnegie made a gift of $10,000,000 to found the Carnegie Institution of Washington—devoted to scientific research. Carnegie, who retired in 1901, during his lifetime gave $60,000,000 for the establishment of free public libraries. Some of his endowments supported educational institutions. Carnegie donated the money to build a Peace Palace for the meetings of world conferences at The Hague in the Netherlands. In 1900, Carnegie wrote *The Gospel of Wealth,* defending the ownership of nearly seventy-five per cent of the nation's wealth by less than ten per cent of the people. He declared that the enterprising few deserved the wealth for making the United States a world leader. Carnegie held that all of the people ultimately benefited as the wealth worked its way down to the masses. Finally, those who amassed great fortunes were able to support philanthropies. Carnegie adhered completely to his conception of the "stewardship" of wealth.

The romance of steel is largely the story of Scotch-born Andrew Carnegie. He came to America as a boy of twelve and soon was earning $1.20 a week at a cotton mill near Pittsburgh. Carnegie became secretary for the general superintendent of the Pennsylvania Railroad. Turning to steel, he installed one of America's first Bessemer converters and over the years built up a steel empire. In 1901, Carnegie sold his multi-million dollar holdings to a group headed by J. P. Morgan, the famous financier. Out of Carnegie's empire came America's first billion-dollar corporation, the United States Steel Corporation—Big Steel.

☆ 737 ☆

1902

CUBA WAS EVACUATED by American troops in March, 1902. Eleven months earlier, the Platt Amendment had been incorporated in Cuba's constitution, giving the United States partial control over the island. The Cubans did not relish the continuing American influence, but the withdrawal of troops was conditional upon it. In the months since accepting the Platt provisions, Cuba had formed its own government. Rule of the island was turned over on May 20 to Cuba's first president by the American military administration, headed by General Wood.

The Platt guarantees later were written into a treaty between the United States and Cuba. Encouraged by this promise of stability, American interests increased their investments in Cuban enterprises. In 1901, these investments totaled $80,000,000 and they multiplied rapidly. Soon many of Cuba's rich sugar plantations were owned by Americans, some of them under the control of banking houses. The Cubans did not like the American financial domination any more than the presence of American troops.

A spirit of nationalism began to develop among the Cubans because of the restrictions. They resented outside influences and seized every opportunity to demonstrate it. After an early period of political tranquility, the Cubans injected fierce partisanship into their elections. Some United States leaders regretted the clause in the declaration of war on Spain which had pledged that this nation would not acquire any Cuban territory and would turn the island's government over to its people. Some newspapers agreed with them that full control over Cuba, or none at all, would have been better.

1902

RHODES SCHOLARSHIPS to Oxford University were created by Cecil Rhodes to spur youths' ambitions for higher education. Rhodes, famed developer and statesman of South Africa, left a huge fortune for endowment of scholarships in British colonies, the United States and Germany. Reading of Rhodes' will on April 4, 1902, following his death in March, revealed that Rhodes left $10,000,000 to provide for the scholarships in America. Versatile male students with two years in an accredited college or university could study at the British institution. Cecil Rhodes hoped that these scholarships to American students would help unite all the English-speaking peoples.

Rhodes joined a brother in South Africa in 1870 when seventeen years old. He followed the rush to newly-discovered diamond fields of Kimberley. Armed with a shovel and a bucket, young Rhodes scooped up a fortune in a few months. In the following years, Rhodes became prime minister of Cape Colony and managing director of the powerful British South Africa Company. Fulfilling an early dream, he divided his time for eight years between attending Oxford and managing his South African interests. Rhodesia in South Africa is named for the founder of the Rhodes Scholarships.

☆ 739 ☆

1902

A "SQUARE DEAL" for labor, management and the public was one of Theodore Roosevelt's proudest mottoes. The United Mine Workers of America asked the President to make good his promise. In May, 1902, the union called a strike of miners in the anthracite coal regions of Pennsylvania. The union demanded that it be recognized and that the workers be granted a twenty per cent wage increase, a nine-hour day, and improved working conditions. The mine owners rejected all demands and refused to arbitrate.

With the arrival of fall and the possibility of a coal shortage, Roosevelt on October 3 invited the union and mine managers to a conference in the White House. President John Mitchell of the miners' union proved cooperative, but the mine owners did not. On October 6, the Pennsylvania National Guard was ordered to the mine fields to prevent riots. President Mitchell kept the miners from violence and thereby won the public's sympathy and support.

Roosevelt threatened to send federal troops "under a first class general" with orders to "dispossess the operators and run the mines as a receiver." The owners then relented and the President named a seven-man commission to settle the dispute. The strike was declared ended and the miners went back to work on October 23. In its later decision, the commission awarded the miners a ten per cent wage increase and a nine-hour day. Although the union was refused recognition, it was hailed as a "square deal."

1902

AMERICA'S GREAT NATURAL resources declined through waste, destruction and neglect. Farm lands, in particular, were hard hit. Millions of acres in the South, West and Southwest no longer were productive and had been abandoned for farming purposes. Congress, which already had launched a preliminary conservation program, took note of the "worn out" lands. On June 17, 1902, the Newlands Reclamation Act was passed —designed to restore old farm lands and open many new ones for varied crops.

The reclamation act provided for proceeds of public land sales in sixteen Southwestern and Western states to be set aside for irrigation purposes. The funds would be used to build and maintain irrigation facilities in arid and semi-arid regions. Networks of water distributing installations were planned. The blueprints called for dams to provide reservoirs of water and tunnels to convey the water to the arid areas. Flumes (troughs) then would distribute the water into ditches serving the thirsty fields. The federal government went into the irrigation business through the reclamation act.

Other natural resources needed conservation measures and Congress already had taken the first steps. Many of America's once thick forests had been chopped thin. Huge lumber companies held contracts to fell more timber on an unrestricted basis. In 1891 Congress passed a Forest Reserve Act which empowered the President to establish forest reserve lands in the public domain. These reserves were to be used for national parks. President Roosevelt, a conservation enthusiast, included continuation of this project in his administration program.

A "GO-AHEAD" ON THE CANAL was authorized by Congress. Following England's granting to the United States of exclusive control, plans went forward for construction of the water passage across the Isthmus of Panama. The matter of a right of way was the primary problem. The French Panama Canal Company, successor to the bankrupt De Lesseps venture, held rights across Panama. An alternate route for the canal lay through Nicaragua. The Roosevelt administration considered both possibilities and decided on Panama as preferable. The French Panama Canal Company, however, asked $109,000,000 for its rights. When the United States balked at the price the French company reconsidered. Its Panama option was scheduled to expire in 1904, when all claims would be lost. The company sliced its price to $40,000,000.

Congress passed the Panama Canal (or Spooner) Act on June 28, 1902. The measure appropriated $40,000,000 for the purchase of the French company's Panama rights and property. Since Panama was a province of Colombia, the act also specified that a grant must be obtained from Colombia for perpetual control of the canal zone. Should negotiations with Colombia fail, efforts then would be made to obtain a Nicaraguan right of way. An Isthmian Canal Commission was created and the first steps were taken toward actual work on the canal project. Secretary of State Hay opened negotiations with Colombia for the necessary agreement.

1902

ORDER IN THE PHILIPPINES was restored and a government for the islands was created by Congress. Despite the earlier capture of the leader, Emilio Aguinaldo, the Filipino insurrection was not crushed until mid-1902. The Philippines then were considered ready for civil government. On July 1, 1902, Congress passed the Philippine Government (Organic) Act which confirmed William H. Taft as governor-general and the Taft Commission as the Philippines' ruling body. The Organic Act made the Philippines an "unorganized territory." Its inhabitants became citizens of the Philippines, but not of the United States. Males over twenty-three were granted suffrage and most of the constitutional guarantees were extended to the Filipinos. At the time the islands were annexed, the Senate adopted the McEnery Resolutions, pledging the United States not to hold the Philippines permanently. The task of Taft was to get the Filipinos started toward self-rule.

The Taft Commission, appointed by Roosevelt, was composed of five Americans and three Filipinos. The population of the islands included 7,000,000 Filipinos, most of them of the Roman Catholic faith. There were many mixed Asiatic races, and savage tribes lurked in the jungles. Taft's administration plunged resolutely into its assignment. Large areas of land were purchased from three Catholic orders and sold to the Filipinos, on easy terms, as small farms. A sanitation program was launched and roads were built. The American system of free schools was installed in the Philippines.

1902

A CRISIS IN THE CARIBBEAN arose over huge debts which Venezuela owed foreign investors. Under dictator Cipriano Castro, Venezuela suffered from civil war and property destruction. Much of the property was owned by citizens of European nations. The Venezuelan government also had borrowed heavily. Castro claimed inability to pay the debts. In 1901, he rejected a proposal by Germany that the matter be referred to the Hague international tribunal for settlement. Great Britain, holding a much larger stake in the debts than Germany, joined the dispute. Only caution generated by the United States' Monroe Doctrine restrained the European powers from dealing swiftly and drastically with Castro.

President Roosevelt was not particularly concerned over the Venezuela quarrel. He had said that disciplining of a delinquent South American republic by a European power did not violate the Monroe Doctrine, as long as it did not involve acquisition of territory. Encouraged by this apparent tolerance, Germany and England blockaded Venezuelan ports in December, 1902, to compel payment of the debts. Several of the republic's warships were seized or sunk. Italian naval vessels joined the blockade. Cipriano Castro's defiance ended and he asked for arbitration by the United States.

Germany's emergence as an empire seeker, with the accession of Wilhelm II to the throne, disturbed Roosevelt. The Germans had attempted to appease the American President by presenting him with a medal. Roosevelt apparently was not influenced by the German overtures. He claimed to have threatened the kaiser with action by the American fleet if the blockade question was not arbitrated. Whether it was Roosevelt's threat or not, the matter was submitted to arbitration on December 12, 1902.

1902

ARGENTINA WAS INDIGNANT over the Venezuela incident. Even though the European fleets had not come close to her own shores, Argentina objected. On December 29, 1902, the Argentine minister of foreign affairs, Luis Drago, sent a note to Washington. He protested that no European power had the right to send armed forces to collect debts owed its citizens by American nations. The document, which became known as the Drago Doctrine, strengthened the Monroe Doctrine. It called for official congressional reaction to the incident.

President Roosevelt by now was concerned over the Caribbean situation and its Monroe Doctrine implications. His statement in his first annual message to Congress in 1901 was remembered. Roosevelt had asserted then that the Monroe Doctrine "did not guarantee any state against punishment if it misconducts itself, provided that punishment does not take the form of acquisition of territory by any non-American power."

But now the picture had changed. An American republic had been punished and another American republic resented it. The United States could not avoid being involved in Latin-American affairs.

German warships, meanwhile, shelled and leveled Fort San Carlos, Venezuela, in January, 1903. The American public roared protest. The New York *Times*, representative of the nation's press reaction, said, "Worse international manners than Germany has exhibited from the beginning of this wretched Venezuela business have rarely come under the observation of civilized man." The British press criticized its government for allying the royal navy with the Germans in the Venezuela adventure. Under the combined pressure, Germany and England decided to leave the matter to arbitration. The Venezuela issue was settled by the Hague tribunal later—but a picture had been drawn of Kaiser Wilhelm as a stern monarch with an upturned mustache, rattling a saber.

1903

INTERSTATE COMMERCE ABUSES came under study by the Roosevelt administration. The Interstate Commerce Act of 1887 had established a code of fair relations between shippers and railroads. But frequent adverse rulings in the federal courts limited the act's powers. Its effectiveness was reduced in numerous cases by vague definitions of what constituted "abuses" and "penalties." One complex issue was the granting by railroads of freight rebates, or discounts, to favored large shippers. The small shippers, required to pay the full rates, were placed at a competitive disadvantage in their interstate commerce.

The Elkins Act was passed by Congress on February 19, 1903. This measure defined clearly the areas of "discrimination" by the railroads between interstate shippers and set specific penalties. The granting or receiving of freight rebates was declared illegal. The railroad officials or agents who gave the rebates, as well as the shippers who accepted them, were equal violators. Railroads which deviated from their posted or published rates were subject to misdemeanor charges. Federal courts were given power to issue injunctions.

The huge trusts seeking to hold monopolies in America's commerce were attacked by the President. Two acts were passed in 1903 aimed at the trusts. The Department of Commerce and Labor was created by Congress with cabinet status. The first Secretary of Commerce and Labor was George B. Cortelyou of New York. Another measure, known as the Expedition Act, gave anti-trust cases priority on federal court dockets. Roosevelt openly declared war on the trusts.

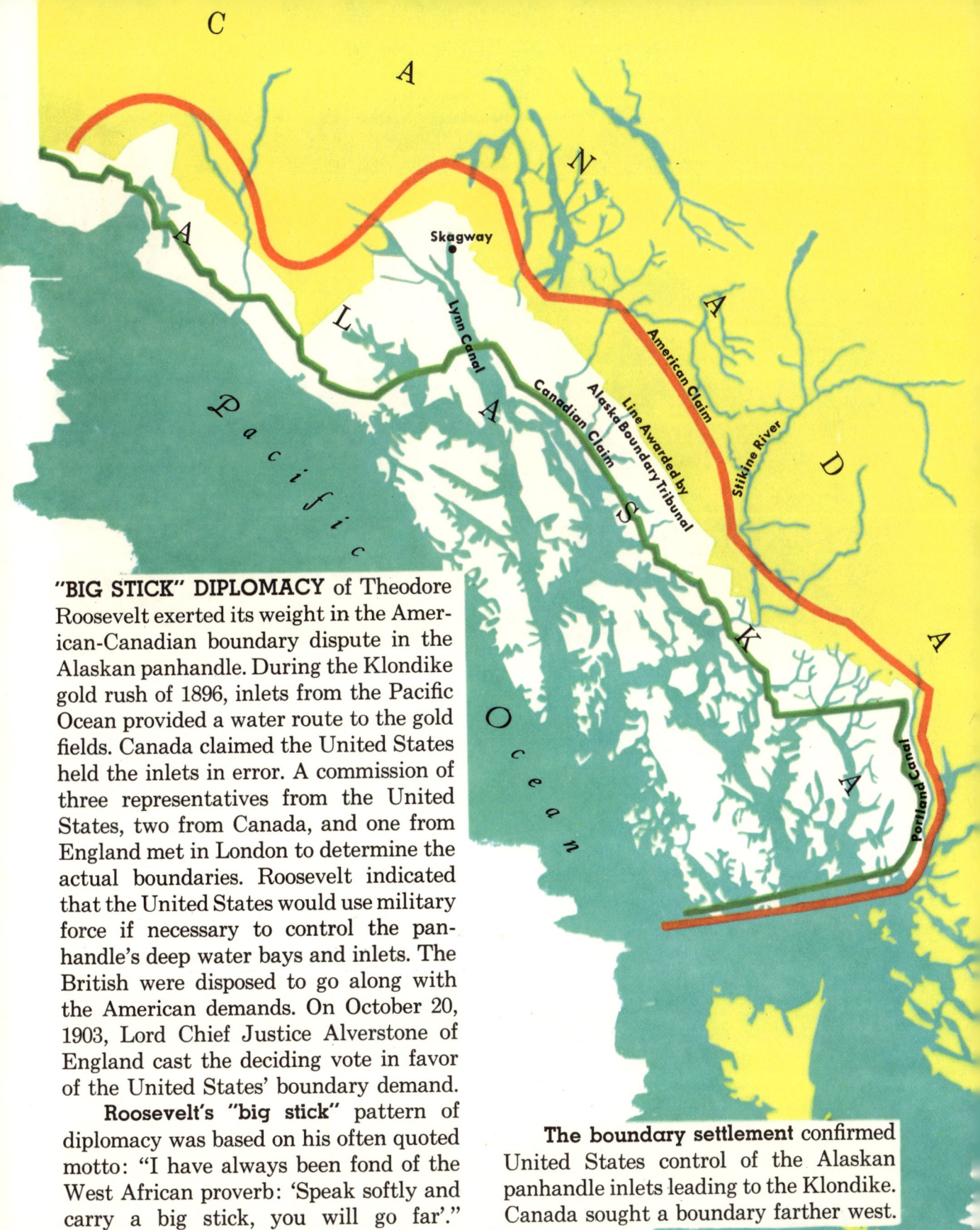

"BIG STICK" DIPLOMACY of Theodore Roosevelt exerted its weight in the American-Canadian boundary dispute in the Alaskan panhandle. During the Klondike gold rush of 1896, inlets from the Pacific Ocean provided a water route to the gold fields. Canada claimed the United States held the inlets in error. A commission of three representatives from the United States, two from Canada, and one from England met in London to determine the actual boundaries. Roosevelt indicated that the United States would use military force if necessary to control the panhandle's deep water bays and inlets. The British were disposed to go along with the American demands. On October 20, 1903, Lord Chief Justice Alverstone of England cast the deciding vote in favor of the United States' boundary demand.

Roosevelt's "big stick" pattern of diplomacy was based on his often quoted motto: "I have always been fond of the West African proverb: 'Speak softly and carry a big stick, you will go far'."

The boundary settlement confirmed United States control of the Alaskan panhandle inlets leading to the Klondike. Canada sought a boundary farther west.

★ 747 ★

1903

AMERICA OBTAINED ITS CANAL right-of-way through a series of diplomatic maneuvers—with military overtones. A treaty was arranged with Colombia in January, 1903, to lease a ten-mile strip across Panama for $10,000,000 cash and $250,000 annual rental. The Colombian senate rejected the treaty, saying it gave the United States too much control for too little compensation. Directors of the French Panama Canal Company were alarmed as they faced the loss of a $40,000,000 sale and expiration of their franchise.

The canal company conveniently had a former associate who was a revolutionist in Panama — Philippe Bunau-Varilla. The company encouraged Bunau-Varilla to incite a Panamanian revolution against Colombia. President Roosevelt, aware of the plan, sent American naval forces to keep the isthmus railroad operating and "to prevent the landing of any armed forces with hostile intent, either government or belligerent." On November 3, the revolution broke out in Panama. The next day, the United States troops landed to block Colombian interference. The revolution was a bloodless success and on November 6 Secretary of State John Hay formally recognized the Republic of Panama as a new nation.

Bunau-Varilla arrived at Washington as Panama's first minister to the United States. On November 18, 1903, the Hay-Bunau-Varilla Treaty was signed. Panama gave the United States perpetual use of a ten-mile Panama Canal strip with full sovereignty and the right to fortify the zone. Panama received the $10,000,000 and annual rental. The French company's rights were purchased. America obtained the Panama Railroad Company for good measure. Colombia's resentment smoldered for many years.

1903

AN AIRPLANE THAT FLEW! Orville and Wilbur Wright, brothers who owned a bicycle shop in Ohio, invented and flew the first successful airplane. On December 17, 1903, they made four flights at Kitty Hawk, North Carolina. Orville Wright made the first flight, keeping the awkward craft in the air for twelve seconds and traveling 120 feet. Wilbur made the longest flight of the day—remaining aloft for fifty-nine seconds and covering 852 feet. Their airplane was the first powered, heavier-than-air craft to fly successfully— although man had been experimenting with the idea for many years.

The Wrights' airplane resembled a box kite. It weighed 750 pounds and was powered by a twelve-horsepower gasoline engine weighing 170 pounds. The pilot lay on the front edge of the lower wing, looking straight down at the ground. Soaring through the air was not new to the Wright brothers. Since 1900, they had been experimenting with a two-man glider at Kitty Hawk. They built a wind tunnel and conducted numerous tests of the air currents' effects on various types of wing surfaces and controls. They developed a scientific formula for flying —and now they proved that it worked.

Returning to Dayton, where they had their shop, the Wrights made successive improvements in their plane. After making a flight of thirty-eight minutes, they obtained a patent in May, 1906. In August, 1909, the United States army accepted the Wrights' airplane following tests at Fort Myer, Virginia. Few newspapers had even mentioned that eventful December day's feat at Kitty Hawk!

☆ 749 ☆

1904

THE "TRUST BUSTER" was another designation applied to Roosevelt as he pushed his fight on monopolies. The President declared his policy, "We do not wish to destroy corporations, but we do wish to make them subserve the public good." The trend toward mergers and holding companies in big business had increased. One of the major fields where mergers had reduced competition was the railroad industry. Six systems controlled about three-fourths of the nation's total railroad track mileage. Roosevelt aimed his campaign at railroad trusts.

On the President's order, Attorney General Philander C. Knox of Pennsylvania entered suit in 1902 against the Northern Securities Company. This was a company formed by J. P. Morgan, James J. Hill and Edward Harriman to control the three main railroads serving the Pacific Northwest from the Great Lakes centers. The roads were the Great Northern, Northern Pacific and the Chicago Burlington and Quincy. The government's suit claimed that the Northern Securities Company's control of the roads merged former competitors into a single non-competitive enterprise. Violation of the Sherman Anti-Trust Act was charged.

The Supreme Court, in a five-to-four decision on March 14, 1904, ruled against the Northern Securities Company and ordered it dissolved. The majority opinion held that Northern Securities strangled free competition in violation of the Sherman Act. The decision strengthened the act as a force against monopolies. While the Northern Securities case was being deliberated, Congress had established a Bureau of Corporations within the Department of Commerce and Labor. The bureau's function was to investigate corporations suspected of trust violations. The Northern Securities decision and the Bureau of Corporations gave "Trust Buster" Roosevelt potent weapons.

1904

ROOSEVELT'S GREAT POPULARITY won his election as President in 1904 by a margin of more than 2,500,000 votes over his Democratic opponent. Roosevelt was chosen by acclamation at the Republican convention in Chicago. Charles W. Fairbanks of Indiana was the choice for Vice-President. The Republican platform was drafted by party conservatives and made bare mention of Roosevelt's aggressive policies. Alton B. Parker, a New York judge, was nominated by the Democrats at St. Louis. Parker insisted upon the Democrats backing the gold standard in their platform, in an appeal for Wall Street support. This reversed the stand of the party's "free silver" leader, William Jennings Bryan. Henry G. Davis of West Virginia was named for Vice-President.

Five other parties nominated candidates. They were: Socialist—Eugene V. Debs of Indiana and Benjamin Hanford of New York; Prohibition—Silas C. Swallow of Pennsylvania and George W. Carroll of Texas; Socialist Labor—Charles H. Corregan of New York; People's (Populist)—Thomas E. Watson of Georgia and Thomas H. Tibbles of Nebraska, and Continental—Austin Holcomb of Georgia and A. King of Missouri. In the popular voting on November 8, 1904, Roosevelt received 7,623,486 votes to Parker's 5,077,911. Debs received 402,460, Swallow 258,536, Watson 117,183, Corregan 41,249 and Holcomb 830.

Roosevelt swept thirty-two states to win 336 electoral votes. Parker won thirteen states for 140 votes. The victory of their "big stick" and "trust buster" champion was jubilantly celebrated by the millions who voted for him. Roosevelt was sworn in for his full term as President by Chief Justice Melville Weston Fuller on March 4, 1905. A huge parade marked the occasion, with more than 200,000 jamming Washington's streets to view the procession. It was a day of triumph for Theodore Roosevelt and he enjoyed it to the fullest. On the night of his election the President had said, "Under no circumstances will I be a candidate for or accept another nomination."

1904

POLICING UNRULY NEIGHBORS in the Caribbean and Latin America was decided upon by Roosevelt as the best guarantee against European intervention. The Dominican Republic became heavily indebted to foreign investors. The country's chief source of revenue was its customhouses. When the Dominican Republic became bankrupt through civil wars, disorders and government graft, Belgium proposed that an international commission take over the customhouses. Roosevelt rejected the suggestion. Then the Dominican Republic gave an American creditor preferred treatment over foreigners. As protests from Europe mounted, the President announced a new policy in his annual message to Congress on December 6, 1904. Roosevelt said: "Chronic wrongdoing, or an impotence which results in a general loosening of the ties of civilized society, may in America, as elsewhere, ultimately require intervention by some civilized nation, and in the Western Hemisphere the adherence of the United States to the Monroe Doctrine may force the United States, however reluctantly, in flagrant cases of such wrongdoing or impotence, to the exercise of an international police power." The declaration became known as the Roosevelt Corollary to the Monroe Doctrine. It proclaimed that the United States could make use of the Monroe Doctrine—which barred interventions—as a means of intervening itself to preserve order in the Western Hemisphere.

1905

LABOR'S GAINS WERE SLOW as the Supreme Court interpreted the Fourteenth Amendment conservatively. Many justices ruled that laws regulating hours, wages and working conditions infringed on an employer's property rights. At the same time, they said, such laws limited the worker's opportunity to decide for himself whether working conditions were satisfactory. This judicial theory was based on "freedom of contract," under the judges' interpretation of the Fourteenth Amendment. Labor disputed the reasoning on the grounds that there was no "freedom." Without regulations, they maintained, management established its own conditions and the workers could accept them or have no jobs at all.

A major case was Lochner vs. New York, in which the Supreme Court voided a New York law creating a ten-hour day in the baking industry. The majority held that the law interfered with the rights of the individual and gave the state illegal "police powers" over employment. Justice Oliver Wendell Holmes dissented. He stated that the New York law was a health measure, providing better conditions for the worker and a better bakery product for the public.

Holmes criticized the majority's voiding of the law as being founded on "an economic theory which a large part of the country does not entertain." He said that the Constitution was "not intended to embody a particular economic theory." The public health and welfare interpretation injected a new viewpoint in labor deliberations. Roosevelt used this point in planning to send federal troops to reopen strike-bound Pennsylvania coal mines in 1902. With winter coming on, public health and welfare were periled by a shortage of coal.

1905

INTERVENTION IN SANTO DOMINGO (Dominican Republic) came after the Roosevelt Corollary. In January, 1905, the Dominican Republic signed an agreement for the United States to put an American financial expert in charge of its bankrupt treasury. The Senate failed to ratify the arrangement, but Roosevelt went ahead on his own. Santo Domingo appointed an administrator nominated by the President. Forty-five per cent of the customs receipts was devoted to the island's governmental expenses. Fifty-five per cent was deposited in New York banks for payment on the debts. With graft eliminated from the customhouses, revenues rose and debts decreased. The people of Santo Domingo became less discontented as they gained security, and revolutionary spirit died out. In February, 1907, the Senate finally ratified a treaty with Santo Domingo on the lines of Roosevelt's original agreement, but by then the crisis was over. Santo Domingo became solvent again and the American control was withdrawn in July, 1907.

Varied reactions came to this application of the Roosevelt Corollary. European powers frowned on America's advance from Monroe Doctrine protection to Corollary intervention, but the continental bankers and investors were pleased. In North America, many applauded Roosevelt, but the Democrats generally denounced the Santo Domingo incident as domineering. In Latin America, there was no particular resentment at that time among the other republics.

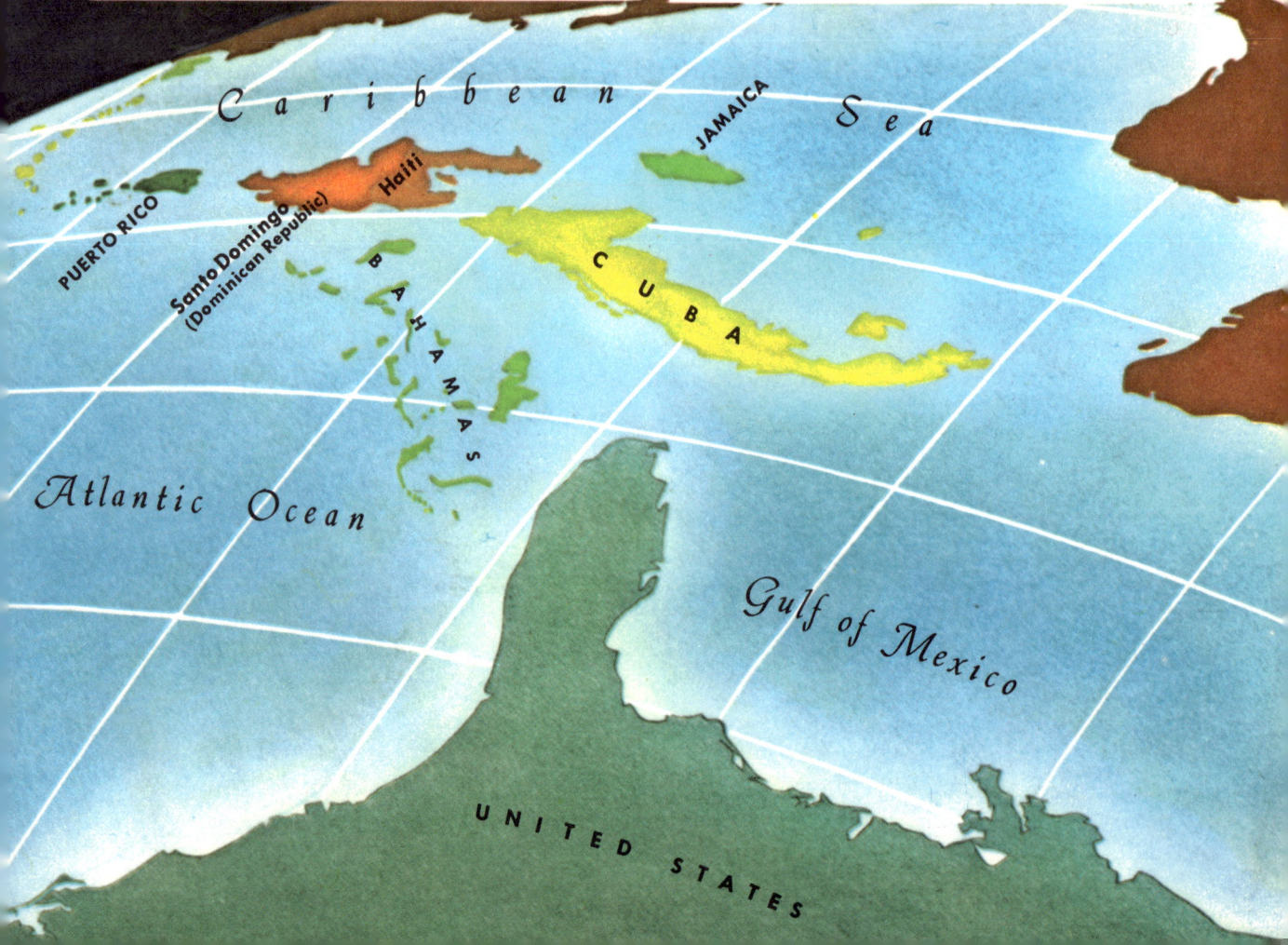

1905

JAPAN DEFEATED RUSSIA in a war over Far Eastern interests. Russia failed to withdraw its troops from the Chinese province of Manchuria after the Boxer Uprising of 1900. Japan feared Russia would seize Manchuria and also Korea, where Japan had her own plans. In February, 1904, the Japanese broke relations.

Without declaring war, Japan launched a surprise attack two days later and defeated a Russian fleet at Port Arthur, Manchuria. The czar sent another fleet around Africa to the war zone. The Russians arrived exhausted from the long cruise at maximum speed. Their supplies were depleted and the crew was in poor condition. The Japanese attacked and also defeated this fleet in the Battle of Tsushima Straits, between Japan and Korea, on May 27-29, 1905. Japan asked Roosevelt to act as mediator to end the war. The United States had vital interests in the Far East, including the Open Door policy in Chinese trade. Roosevelt did not want the balance of power to be broken in the Orient. He accepted the role of peacemaker and Russia finally agreed. A Russian-Japanese peace treaty was signed at the Portsmouth, New Hampshire, navy yard on August 9, 1905. Japan acquired Russia's leasehold in Manchuria and the South Manchurian railroad. Also, Japanese domination over Korea was recognized. Japanese demands **for cash indemnity from Russia were** blocked by Roosevelt, but Japan was given the southern half of the island of Sakhalin north of the Japanese islands. The Taft-Katsura Memorandum was signed prior to the conference. The United States agreed not to interfere with Japanese aims in Korea and Japan promised to undertake no territorial conquests in the Philippines. For mediating the Russian-Japanese dispute, Roosevelt was awarded the Nobel Peace Prize in 1906.

1906

EUROPEAN RIVALRIES turned into smoldering enmities as the race for empires and world power quickened. In 1904, England and France signed an Entente Cordiale (friendly agreement) recognizing their respective interests in Egypt and Morocco. France desired to establish a protectorate in Morocco, an independent North African state ruled by a sultan. France also negotiated with Spain and Italy to have them agree to the protectorate. In return, England, Spain and Italy were to have their particular interests recognized elsewhere in North Africa.

Kaiser Wilhelm II of Germany was opposed to the arrangement. In March, 1905, he made a defiant speech at Tangier in which he proclaimed Germany's support of Morocco's independence. The kaiser asked Roosevelt's aid in arranging a conference on Morocco with England and France. The President was reluctant to deviate from America's established policy of not interfering in European affairs. But Roosevelt was convinced that Europe's antagonisms could blaze into a world war involving the United States.

France and England agreed to meet with Germany, at Roosevelt's urging. The conference opened at Algeciras, Spain, in January, 1906. Henry White attended as senior American delegate. The Act of Algeciras was signed on April 7. It recognized the independence of Morocco and guaranteed equal commercial rights to all nations. An international bank was created to help Morocco stabilize its finances. The French and Spanish were given control of the Moroccan police. The Senate ratified the convention, but qualified the approval by reiterating America's "hands off" European policy.

1906

JOURNALISTIC CRUSADERS who specialized in exposing greed and graft were given the name of "muckrakers" by Roosevelt. Some magazines and special writers conducted sensational campaigns on trusts, politics and dishonest business practices. They wrote vivid articles, arousing Americans' indignation—and increasing the sales of their publications. In a speech on April 14, 1906, Roosevelt took note of the trend of the reform writers and referred to them as "muckrakers." He made the comparison from the character in *Pilgrim's Progress* "who could look no way but downward with the muckrake in his hands." The name clung, although Roosevelt was, in general, sympathetic with aims of the writers.

Among the national magazines which built up circulation with the exposes were *McClure's*, *Everybody's*, *Cosmopolitan*, *Collier's*, *American*, *Pearson's* and *Munsey's*. Typical of the "muckraking" stories, and their authors, were: *Frenzied Finance* by Thomas Lawson, *The History of the Standard Oil Company* by Ida M. Tarbell, *The Octopus* and *The Pit* by Frank Norris, and *The Railroads on Trial*, by Ray Stannard Baker. *The Treason of the Senate* was written by David Graham Phillips. Lincoln Steffen's *Shame of the Cities* described corruption in local government. Upton Sinclair wrote about conditions in Chicago's stockyards and meat packing plants in his novel, *The Jungle*. Another significant book on the meat industry was *The Greatest Trust in the World* by Charles Edward Russell. The "muckrakers" won popular support in an era marked by clamor for reform.

1906

A MIGHTY EARTHQUAKE struck San Francisco on April 18, 1906, and all America shuddered under the impact of the tragedy. A deep internal convulsion of the earth was accompanied by some of San Francisco's streets being split into chasms. Tall buildings swayed and toppled. Walls crumpled and roofs crashed. Timbers, bricks, panes of glass and other debris were flung through the air. Fire broke out from the ruins and swept the city. The residents were panic stricken. Thousands of people, suddenly finding themselves without shelter, stampeded through the streets. The fire raged for three days. Areas were dynamited in an effort to check the flames. More than four square miles of the city were destroyed. Only one mansion on Nob Hill, residential section of the wealthy, remained undamaged. After the flames subsided, it was found that 452 people had been killed, thousands injured, and property damage of $350,000,000 had been caused by the earthquake and fire. As soon as communications were reestablished, San Francisco sent out an appeal for help. The entire nation responded in an outpouring of sympathy. Special trains were rushed to the stricken city, carrying doctors, nurses, workingmen, tools, materials, food, clothing and medical supplies. Money from earthquake relief funds poured in. San Francisco arose from the ruins, squared its shoulders, and in four years the city was rebuilt.

1906

Pure Food And Drug Act Guarded Public Against Tainted Products

Congress passed the Pure Food and Drug Act on June 30, 1906. Abuses and malpractices exposed by the "muckrakers" helped inspire the measure to protect public health.

The act was aimed at the manufacturers of processed foods, meat companies and producers of drugs and patent medicines. It required inspections in interstate sales.

Harmful preservatives, adulteration and misbranding were barred.

Inspections were ordered for all meats sold across state lines, according to a Meat Inspection Act.

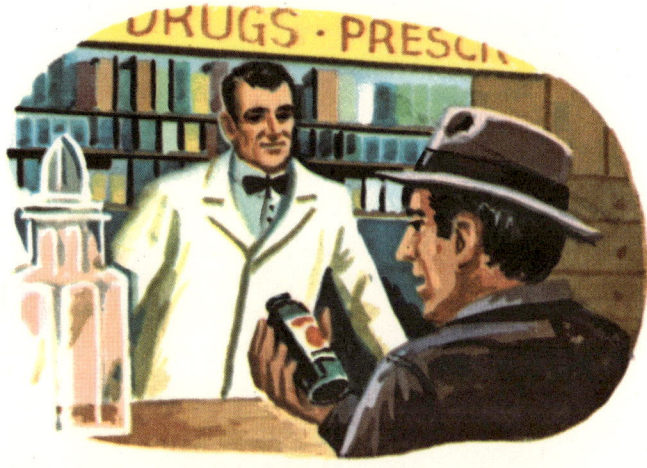

Habit-forming drugs were barred from use in patent medicines. Labels had to state the exact contents.

☆ 759 ☆

1907

BUILDING OF THE PANAMA CANAL finally got under way in earnest in 1907 with the appointment of the army's Lieutenant Colonel George Washington Goethals as the chief engineer. Preliminary work, begun in 1905, was halted by the first of many difficult problems. An outbreak of yellow fever and malaria resulted in a high death rate among the canal employes. Colonel William C. Gorgas brought the fever under control by employing the same methods which had cleaned up Havana. When the Gorgas sanitation program was completed, the long-term project could be started. A lock canal, instead of a sea-level passage, was decided upon and, on April 1, 1907, Roosevelt signed a bill which authorized full scale construction. The project was placed under the Secretary of War—William H. Taft at the time. The Canal Commission was reorganized, eliminating divided authority, and Goethals was given complete charge. Many major problems remained, including engineering decisions, housing, employee relations and law enforcement. Goethals, with a splendid record as an officer of the United States Army Engineering Corps, solved them all. As he continued to demonstrate his administrative ability, Goethals was promoted to colonel (later major general). The canal began to take shape. Excavations progressed on schedule and the canal zone became a scene of bustling activity. Thousands of workers moved in with their families and were housed. Step by step, the Panama Canal stretched over its 50.4-mile length from Cristobal on the Caribbean Sea to Balboa on the Bay of Panama on the Pacific side.

1907

ACROSS THE ATLANTIC IN FIVE DAYS! Fastest and finest steamship afloat was the *Lusitania* when the luxury liner made her maiden voyage in 1907. Pride of the British Cunard Line, the *Lusitania* sailed from Queenstown, Ireland, determined to set a new speed record for an Atlantic crossing. Her more than 2,000 passengers were in a gay and excited holiday mood. The marine engineers who designed the *Lusitania* gave her a new and revolutionary type of steam turbine. The engineers had promised the owners that this ship, the *Lusitania*, could outrace them all!

On the last night out, the officers of the proud *Lusitania* were confident of success. The great new ship was running several hours ahead of the Atlantic record then held by Germany's *Deutschland*. The traditional "last night" celebration of the passengers was particularly jubilant. The next day the *Lusitania* slid into New York harbor to the din of the shrieking whistles of many vessels in the bay. The *Lusitania* had done it! She had crossed the Atlantic in five days and fifty-four minutes. The *Deutschland's* record was five days, seven hours and thirty-eight minutes.

The Lusitania set a new style in luxury steamship travel. The Cunarder was equipped with many innovations—elevators, electrification throughout, cabin telephones, lavish lounges and dining rooms, and numerous recreational features. The turbines soon became the motive power for all large new ships. Great Britain was the leader in the race for ocean passenger ship supremacy in the early 1900's. Among her other famous liners were the *City of Paris*, *Eltruria*, *Teutonic*, *Campania* and *Lucania*.

1907

NEW PLEAS FOR WORLD PEACE were made at the Second International Conference at the Hague, Netherlands. The threat of a general war hung over the world as the Great Powers vied for prestige. The second conference was formally called by the czar of Russia. Roosevelt originally had suggested a meeting in 1904, but the Russo-Japanese War prevented its being held. The second conference opened at the Hague in June, 1907. Forty-six nations sent delegates.

Roosevelt, now firmly entrenched in his role as peacemaker, instructed the American envoys to sponsor the creation of an international court of justice. Disputing nations could take their quarrels to this world court for arbitration. The proposal ended in failure, with the central powers of Europe leading the opposition. The conference adopted fourteen agreements, but twelve of them concerned methods of conducting rather than preventing war. These included regulations for land, sea and aerial warfare. Efforts to "humanize" war were attempted through the banning of such weapons as poison gas. Even the war control measures failed to gain needed ratification by all of the nations.

One major gain was salvaged by the United States from the generally fruitless conference. A revised version of the Drago Doctrine was accepted by The Hague tribunal. This was the Argentine doctrine that European nations could not use armed force to collect debts owed their nationals by American republics. Roosevelt's peace efforts were acclaimed in America, which was well aware of the potential world war powder kegs—such as the Russo-Japanese War, France's adventures in Morocco, as well as Germany's constant aggressiveness.

1908

A LABOR UNION RAN AFOUL of the anti-trust law in boycotting hats made by a manufacturer in Danbury, Connecticut. In 1902, the Hatters' Union engaged in a dispute with D. E. Loewe and Company over the closed shop employing only union members. The company refused a union demand that the closed shop be recognized. The Hatters' Union promoted a nationwide boycott of Loewe's goods by its affiliated units. The company took the case to court, charging that the Sherman Anti-Trust law, barring restraint of trade, had been violated.

The case dragged through the lower courts for several years. Finally, on February 3, 1908, the Supreme Court issued a notable decision. By unanimous opinion, the court ruled that the union had violated the anti-trust law. By forming a combination of labor unions to boycott Loewe's merchandise, the verdict decreed, the hatters were "in restraint of trade." The Loewe company was awarded damages three times the actual losses claimed. The company set the value of sales lost through the boycott at $80,000; the union ultimately was to pay $234,000.

The Danbury Hatters Case was a severe blow to organized labor. It was the first time that the Sherman Anti-Trust Act was applied against a labor union. The law, originally designed to curb trusts and monopolies by business, also was interpreted in the Hatters case as regulating the activities of workers. Interstate boycotts were placed out of reach of the unions as weapons in their disputes with management. Even on the local level, boycotts were considered dangerous tactics by many labor leaders.

1908

SPECTER OF THE "YELLOW PERIL" rose to haunt America's foreign relations. Japan's defeat of Russia inspired conjecture that the Japanese some day might have to be fought, most likely in the Philippines. Immediately at hand was an increasing cheap labor problem—by 1906 Japanese laborers were pouring into the United States at the rate of 1,000 a month. By terms of an 1894 treaty, emigration of their respective citizens was granted by the United States and Japan. But now Japanese immigration into the United States was getting out of hand. Some American editors, led by William Randolph Hearst, summed it up as the "Yellow Peril."

California, once the scene of similar problems in regard to the Chinese, again was heavily invaded. West Coast labor leaders formed a Japanese and Korean Exclusion League. The San Francisco school board segregated Japanese, Chinese and Korean children into a special oriental school. Japan protested that this violated the immigration provisions of the 1894 treaty. Roosevelt invited the San Francisco school board to Washington. The board agreed to rescind its order on the President's promise to seek a method to curb Japanese immigration.

Roosevelt made the famous "Gentlemen's Agreement" with the Japanese. This was an exchange of diplomatic notes. In 1908 Japan agreed not to issue passports to laborers who planned to migrate to the United States. America's right to refuse admittance to Japanese bearing passports to any other nation than the United States was conceded. Through American diplomacy, a "touchy" international matter was temporarily settled.

1908

RAPID PROGRESS WAS MADE in the program for conservation of America's natural resources. In May, 1908, President Roosevelt called a conservation conference at the White House. The governors of thirty-four states attended, as did cabinet members, Supreme Court justices and many congressmen. Also present were such national leaders as Grover Cleveland, William Jennings Bryan, Andrew Carnegie, James J. Hill and John Mitchell. As an outcome of the conference, Roosevelt appointed a Commission on Conservation. Gifford Pinchot of Pennsylvania was named chairman of the group, which included fifty-seven members. The conservation movement gathered speed and scope. Commissions were formed in forty-one states. A survey was made of the nation's forest, water, mineral and soil resources. A report was submitted to Roosevelt which gave the first comprehensive summary of America's natural resources. On becoming President in 1901, Roosevelt had said that conservation was one of America's vital problems. He adopted and vigorously supported a conservation policy and by the end of his administration much had been accomplished. More than 148,000,000 acres of forest lands were set aside as national reserves, as well as approximately 80,000,000 acres of mineral lands. A system of national parks was started.

1908

WILLIAM HOWARD TAFT was elected the twenty-seventh President of the United States in 1908. He was the personal choice of Theodore Roosevelt, who had declared against running for another term. Taft, fifty-one years old, was the sixth President born in the state of Ohio.

The Republicans chose James S. Sherman of New York for Vice-President. They based their campaign on continued support of Roosevelt's policies, including conservation. The Republicans also pledged a reduction in tariffs. For the third time, William Jennings Bryan was nominated by the Democrats, with John W. Kern of Indiana as his running mate. By now Bryan had given up the fight for free silver. He centered his attack on high tariffs and monopoly. Bryan also favored government control of the railroads. Since no crucial issues divided the two major parties, the campaign was dull. The real attraction of William Howard Taft was his close ties with the very popular outgoing President Roosevelt.

Taft was elected over Bryan with 7,679,006 popular votes to 6,409,106, a margin of 1,269,900. Taft received 321 electoral votes from twenty-nine states and Bryan received 162 from seventeen. Taft was a key member of Roosevelt's administration. The Ohio lawyer and former judge had been governor general of the Philippines, provisional governor of Cuba, and Secretary of War.

TENSION IN THE PACIFIC was eased when the United States and Japan reached an understanding on their respective aims. Japan was interested in developing its sphere of influence in southern Manchuria and in Korea. America was determined to maintain the Open Door in China and preserve the Philippines for ultimate independence. Each nation was desirous of expanding its Far Eastern commerce freely and without running constant risk of conflict. Secretary of State Root and Japanese Ambassador Takahira reached an agreement at Washington aimed at avoiding trouble.

The Root-Takahira agreement, signed on November 30, 1908, pledged each nation to maintain the "existing status quo" in the Pacific. Both would uphold the Open Door. The independence and integrity of China was recognized. The United States and Japan would respect their individual territorial "spheres" in the Far East. Should any threat to the "status quo" arise, they would consult with one another on the best method of coping with it. The conditions were outlined in a mutual exchange of notes.

The pressure thus was taken off strained diplomatic relations. But an undercurrent of bitterness persisted in Japan. Following the school segregation incident in San Francisco, laws were passed in some American states prohibiting Japanese from owning property within their boundaries. One leading newspaper in Japan said editorially, "Stand up, Japanese nation! Our countrymen have been humiliated on the other side of the Pacific." Relations between the United States and Japan at no time became completely tranquil.

1909

AMERICA'S NAVAL MIGHT was displayed in a cruise around the world by the entire battleship fleet. Roosevelt ordered the demonstration to impress other powers, particularly Japan. He said, "The United States will no more submit to bullying than it will bully." Sixteen battleships under command of Rear Admiral Robley D. Evans sailed from Hampton Roads, Virginia, in December, 1907. They circled South America, creating good will. When the fleet reached San Francisco, Roosevelt announced it would continue around the world, under command of Rear Admiral Charles S. Sperry. Japan, Australia and other nations invited the fleet to visit their ports, and Roosevelt accepted. Instead of hostility, an enthusiastic welcome greeted the fleet in Japan. Children sang *The Star Spangled Banner* in English. The battleship armada steamed back to Hampton Roads on February 21, 1909—just in time to mark the end of Roosevelt's administration with an exciting flourish of the "big stick."

1909

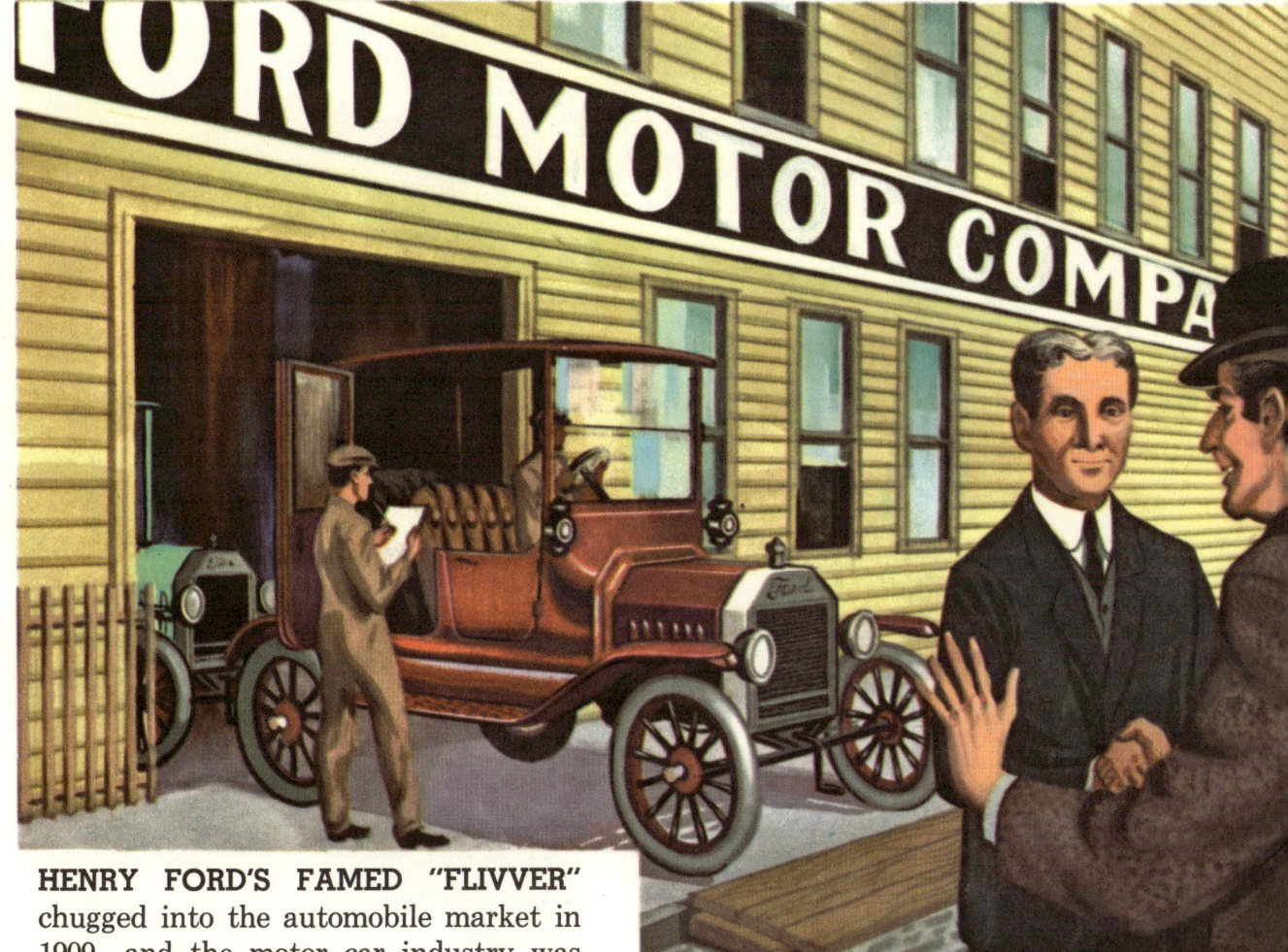

HENRY FORD'S FAMED "FLIVVER" chugged into the automobile market in 1909—and the motor car industry was revolutionized. Called the "Model-T," Ford's ungainly little automobile fulfilled his dream of a "good low-cost car for the people." The "flivver" was not designed for style or good looks, but it was cheap, sturdy and would run. Its gears were controlled by pedals. Ford sold hundreds of thousands of the "Model-T" cars. It was Ford's methods of production—not the car—that revolutionized the automobile industry. Ford adopted a standardized system using interchangeable parts. He introduced the mass production assembly line in the building of cars and the "flivvers" rolled off the factory line in a steady stream.

Henry Ford began work as an apprentice in a Detroit machine shop while a youth of sixteen. He gained experience as a farm machinery repair man. After operating a sawmill, he was employed by the Edison Illuminating Company. Ford next joined the Detroit Automobile Company, which produced custom-built cars. He built his first car in 1902 and the next year organized the Ford Motor Company. Ford was sued by the Association of Licensed Automobile Manufacturers over the first automobile patent, obtained by George B. Selden in 1879. Ford won out in 1911, freeing the industry for unhampered automobile production.

1909

THE NORTH POLE WAS REACHED by Commander Robert Edwin Peary on April 6, 1909. It was the sixth attempt by the United States naval officer and Arctic explorer to reach the pole located at precisely ninety degrees north. In the final and successful effort, Peary led a small party across a vast wasteland of snow and ice. Accompanying him were a Negro servant, Matthew Henson, and four Eskimos. They started from Cape Columbia, Ellesmere Land, on March 1, traveling with sledges drawn by forty dogs. Thirty-seven days later they reached the pole. They crossed the ninety-degree point four times, then built an igloo at the pole. Peary and his followers spent thirty-six hours in the area before starting their return trip. On arriving at Labrador, Peary announced his discovery, only to learn that Doctor Frederick A. Cook claimed he had discovered the North Pole on April 21, 1908. A bitter controversy raged over the respective rights of Peary and Cook to recognition as the first man actually to reach the North Pole. The scientific world finally awarded the distinction to Peary. He was given medals and diplomas by scientific societies. The navy rewarded Peary by promoting him to rear admiral. In an exploration in 1886, he had penetrated the icy interior of Greenland, then virtually unknown territory. Peary reached the Greenland ice cap, 100 miles inland at an elevation of 7,500 feet.

A BROKEN CAMPAIGN PROMISE was charged in the first year of Taft's administration. Prior to the election of 1908, the Republicans pledged a reduction in the heavy Dingley tariffs. True to the promise, Taft asked Congress to revise the tariffs. The result was the Payne-Aldrich Tariff Act, passed on August 5, 1909. Although the tariff average was reduced to about thirty-eight per cent, the duties on numerous specific items were increased. The House had passed a generally reduced tariff, but Senator Nelson W. Aldrich of Rhode Island virtually rewrote the act. Aldrich, finance committee chairman, succeeded in adding 847 amendments—all raising rates.

Taft signed the Payne-Aldrich bill and immediately came under the fire of the "muckrakers." He was accused of flagrant violation of promises. The Republicans were assailed as bowing to the big money interests. Taft made a 13,000-mile speaking tour to explain his stand. At Winona, Minnesota, he made an ill-advised speech calling the tariff "the best the Republicans ever passed."

The President's reputation as a progressive was doomed and his popularity went into decline. Republican Progressives, led by Senator Robert M. La Follette of Wisconsin, bitterly criticized Taft. Speaker of the House Joseph G. Cannon of Illinois, a conservative leader, was drawn into the controversy. He was accused of using his powers as Speaker to block progressive legislation in committees. A bloc headed by Senator George W. Norris of Nebraska succeeded in taking away Cannon's authority to appoint House committees. Republican Progressives were engaged in angry revolt!

Land Reserves Were Restored To Public Sale;

Louis R. Glavis, a special field agent of the Department of the Interior, criticized Ballinger. He claimed that his superior had restored the reserves to favor certain moneyed interests and corporations. Taft ordered Glavis dismissed from the government service. The "muckrakers" launched an attack on the President, charging that he was sabotaging former President Roosevelt's conservation program. Glavis wrote an article for *Collier's* in which he asserted that Ballinger had restored the Alaska coal lands to benefit certain mining interests. Ballinger had handled some legal matters in connection with Alaskan coal lands and therefore knew the area.

LARGE AREAS OF LAND were set aside as conservation reserves during the closing weeks of Roosevelt's administration. These lands—located in Wyoming, Montana and Utah—contained many water power sites. Coal mining lands in Alaska also were removed from public sale and private ownership. On becoming President, Taft removed Roosevelt's Secretary of the Interior, James R. Garfield, and replaced him with Richard A. Ballinger, The new secretary, a lawyer, decided the setting aside of the particular lands was illegal. Ballinger restored them to public sale, available for ownership by private individuals or corporations.

☆ 772 ☆

Taft Accused Of Sabotaging Conservation

Gifford Pinchot, who was named forestry chief under Roosevelt, defended Glavis. He also accused Ballinger of damaging the conservation program by making the former reserves again available to big timber companies and mining corporations. On January 6, 1910, Senator Jonathan Dolliver, a member of the group of Republican progressives opposing Taft, read a Pinchot letter in the Senate. The next day, the President dismissed Pinchot from his post on the grounds of disloyalty as he had forbidden subordinates to correspond directly with Congress on conservation and all similar matters.

The breach widened between Taft and Republican liberals. The adverse publicity created the public impression of Taft as an anti-conservationist. A joint congressional committee conducted an investigation of Ballinger's actions and a majority exonerated him because of inconclusive evidence. Ballinger subsequently resigned in an effort to rescue Taft from political embarrassment, but the damage had been done. Taft's popularity sank lower and a political break with Roosevelt was soon in the making.

1910

THE BOY SCOUTS OF AMERICA grew as a movement to sponsor character, citizenship and physical fitness in American youth. The organization was incorporated on February 8, 1910, and later was granted a charter by Congress. Various earlier boys' groups encouraged interest in outdoor living, self-reliance and patriotism. The first Boy Scouts were organized in the British Empire by Sir Robert Baden-Powell in 1908. Baden-Powell had a friend in America who also was an organizer and leader in Scoutcraft—Daniel Carter Beard, born in the state of Ohio and raised in Kentucky.

Beard, as editor of *Recreation* magazine, organized the Sons of Daniel Boone. Later he formed the Boy Pioneers and wrote *The American Boys' Handbook*. Theodore Roosevelt, then President, was deeply interested in Beard's work with boys. He invited Beard to a conference in Washington and encouraged expansion of the movement. Meanwhile, William D. Boyce, a Chicago publisher, visited England and returned enthusiastic about Scouting. Organization of the Boy Scouts of America followed. Ernest Thompson Seton, nature writer, the first Chief Scout, wrote the *Scouting Handbook*.

The Boy Scout movement grew rapidly. Local councils were formed and churches, schools and community groups sponsored units. Honor is the Boy Scout's guiding creed. The Scout oath says: "On my honor, I will do my best to do my duty to God and my country, and to obey Scout law; to help other people at all times; to keep myself physically strong, mentally awake and morally straight." The Boy Scout motto is "Be prepared."

1910

ROOSEVELT RETURNED from a big game hunt in Africa and found America in political turmoil. Under sponsorship of the Smithsonian Institution, the former President went on the long-anticipated trip soon after the close of his administration. He spent many months hunting and exploring in eastern Africa, and then toured extensively in Europe. On emerging from the jungles, Roosevelt had been met in Egypt by Pinchot, who gave a complete report on the Ballinger controversy. Roosevelt had left the United States confident that Taft would carry on his policies. He returned on June 18, 1910, filled with misgivings. At Osawatomie, Kansas, Roosevelt made a speech on August 31 in which he outlined his principles under a program called New Nationalism. The former President valiantly sought to heal the breach in Republican ranks before the fall congressional elections, but for once the public did not heed his persuasion. The Democrats won a sweeping victory in the elections. They gained control of the House for the first time in sixteen years, winning 229 seats to 161 retained by the Republicans. The Democrats did not win the Senate, but counted on cooperation of the Republican progressive rebels for control. Twenty-six states elected Democratic governors—among them Woodrow Wilson of New Jersey.

1911

DOLLARS INSTEAD OF BULLETS became the ammunition for diplomatic guns which Taft employed to quell new troubles in Latin America. Nicaragua, needing financial help, elected a president friendly to the United States, Adolfo Diaz. An agreement was signed in June, 1911, giving the United States the right to intervene should any foreign nation attempt to control an isthmian canal route across Nicaragua. In return, the United States was to pay the republic's national debt with control over the customhouses of Nicaragua as collateral.

Philander C. Knox, Taft's Secretary of State, made the agreement, but the Senate failed to ratify it. In July, Nicaragua defaulted on its debt to a British syndicate and was desperately in need of funds. Taft, employing "dollar diplomacy," negotiated personally with a group of New York bankers to advance the necessary $1,500,000. The American group was given control of the National Bank of Nicaragua and of the government-owned railroad. In effect, Taft established a financial protectorate over Nicaragua.

The Nicaraguan public objected to the Americans' domination of their treasury and staged a revolution in 1912. A force of United States Marines was sent to the republic to protect American interests. The revolt subsided, but detachments of Marines were stationed in Nicaragua for many years. Taft employed similar "dollar diplomacy" in Honduras, when American bankers provided the funds to cover foreign debts of the republic. An earlier effort to interest United States bankers in backing the construction of a railroad in Manchuria failed—to the embarrassment of Taft and Knox. When both Japan and Russia frowned on the venture, the bankers withdrew. Japan and Russia promptly signed a treaty outlining their respective spheres of influence in Manchuria—in what seemed to be defiance of the Open Door.

1912

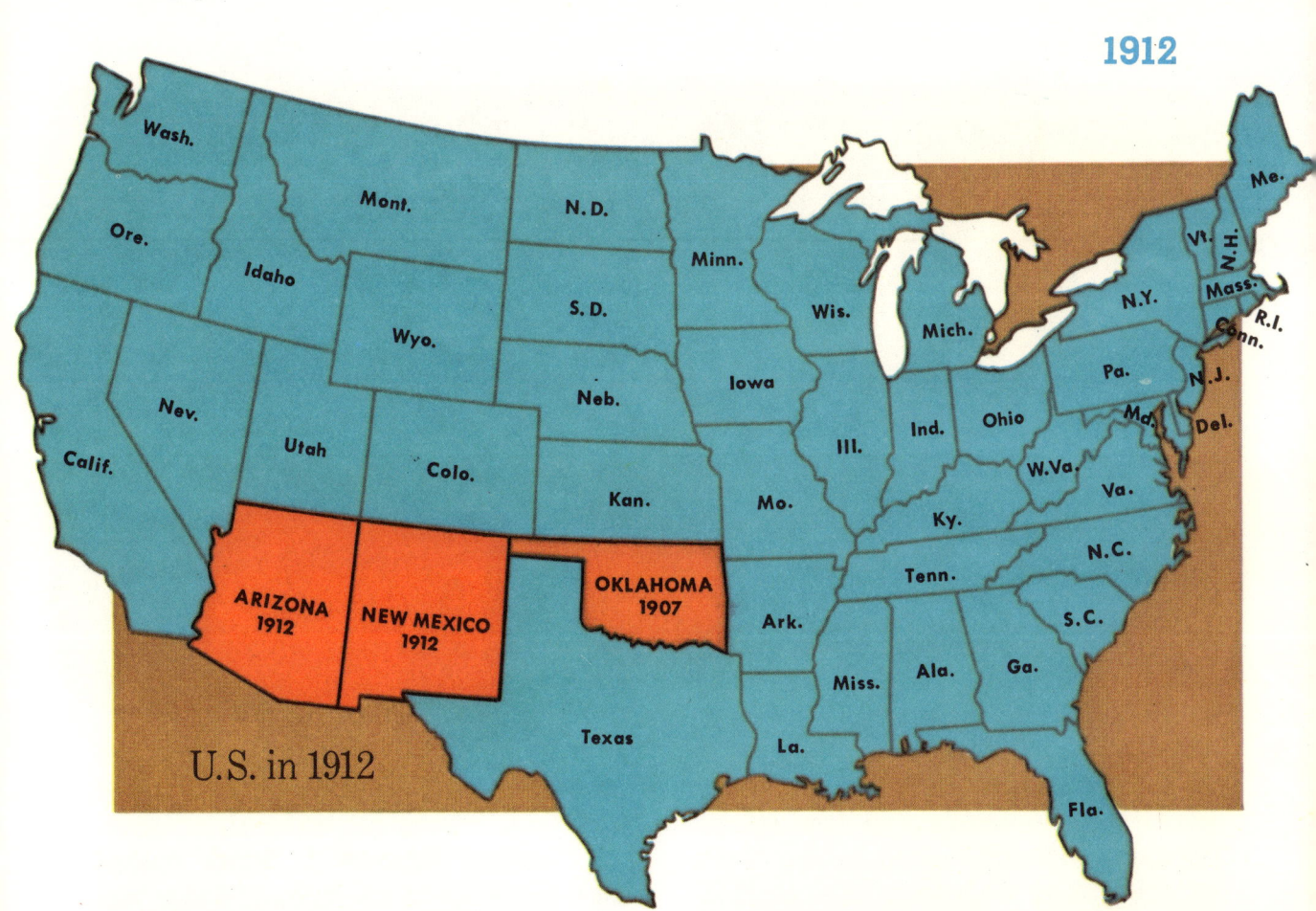

U.S. in 1912

NEW MEXICO AND ARIZONA were admitted in 1912 as the forty-seventh and forty-eighth states of the Union. This left only Alaska as a continental possession not, as yet, admitted as a state. Alaska was given territorial status the same year New Mexico and Arizona became states. Congress adopted joint resolutions on January 6, 1912, to admit New Mexico and Arizona. Taft signed the New Mexico resolution, but vetoed Arizona's admission. The President objected to a clause in Arizona's constitution approving recall of judges (removal from their posts), as a curb on judicial independence.

Arizona eliminated the provision and was admitted on February 14. The state's legislature then amended the constitution, restoring judicial recall. All of the new Western states had adopted progressive constitutions. Both Montana and Arizona provided for referendums and direct primaries. Short terms were decreed for elected officials and executive powers were limited. Women were granted the right to vote in those states.

The trend toward labor and social reforms was reflected in various laws passed in other states. At this time, Massachusetts adopted an act setting up a commission to establish minimum wage rates for working women and children. In 1911, Illinois became the first state to establish a system of public assistance for mothers with dependent children. Earlier, the state of Oregon had passed a law creating a ten-hour work day for all women employed in industry. The first workmen's compensation (payment for injury) act was adopted in Maryland.

1912

SINKING OF THE TITANIC after the luxury liner struck an iceberg off Newfoundland was one of the world's greatest maritime disasters. The huge new British White Star steamship, on her maiden voyage from Southampton to New York, hit the iceberg a glancing blow at 11:40 o'clock at night on April 14, 1912. A hole 300 feet long was gouged in her side. Less than three hours later—at 2:20 the next morning—the *Titanic* sank with most of her 2,223 passengers and crew still aboard. The loss of life was estimated at 1,517.

The Titanic, equipped with water-tight compartments, was called "unsinkable." Grossing 46,328 tons, the 882-foot liner was one of the largest afloat. Lookouts high in the *Titanic*'s superstructure sighted the iceberg dead ahead a few minutes before the collision. "Iceberg!" they shouted over the telephone to the bridge. "All engines stop—full speed astern," the chief officer on the bridge signaled the engine room. The helmsman swung the wheel. The *Titanic*'s bow veered sharply to the left. A towering mass of ice slid by, scraping the side of the ship. A grinding jolt told the officer that the crash had not been avoided. He pressed a button, closing all water-tight doors.

Captain Edward J. Smith rushed from his cabin to the bridge. Water was pouring into the ship on the gouged side. The *Titanic* soon began to list. The captain ordered the passengers into lifeboats—"women and children first." Distress calls started other ships racing to the rescue. One small liner, the *Californian*, was within ten miles, but failed to receive the signal. Scenes of grief and heroism marked the *Titanic*'s final hour ... wives forced to leave husbands and enter lifeboats ... men helping the women and children into the boats ... others leaping into the sea in lifejackets ... Captain Smith and his crew calmly aiding all. As the *Titanic* sank, the ship's band was still playing—many survivors said the last selection was "Nearer My God to Thee." The Cunard liner *Carpathia* succeeded in rescuing 706 survivors of the *Titanic* catastrophe and took them to New York.

1912

TAFT WAS RENOMINATED by the Republicans at their national convention opening at Chicago on June 18, 1912. The national committee, controlled by conservatives, refused to admit certain delegations which included many Roosevelt supporters. The excluded Progressives protested indignantly. The Republicans also renominated Vice-President James S. Sherman, but he died the following October 30. The Republican platform promised stricter control of trusts, a lighter tariff and conservation support.

Theodore Roosevelt became the standard bearer of a new Progressive Party formed by the Republican insurgents. On June 22, this faction held a protest meeting and denounced Taft's renomination as a fraud. Roosevelt said, "If you wish me to make the fight, I will make it, even if only one state should support me." The Progressives definitely wanted Roosevelt and formally nominated him at a later Chicago convention. Hiram W. Johnson of California was named for Vice-President. To match the Republican elephant and Democratic donkey, the Progressives chose a bull moose as their emblem and party nickname. Roosevelt once had boasted proudly, "I feel as strong as a bull moose."

Woodrow Wilson, governor of New Jersey, was nominated by the Democrats, meeting at Baltimore on June 25. Beauchamp (Champ) Clark of Missouri led in the early balloting until William Jennings Bryan switched his support to Wilson. The Democrats nominated Wilson on the forty-sixth ballot. Thomas R. Marshall was chosen for Vice-President. The Democrats asked the abolition of monopolies and a tariff for revenue only.

☆ 779 ☆

1912

WOODROW WILSON WAS ELECTED after an exciting campaign fight. He became the twenty-eighth President. Wilson was a "minority" winner in the popular voting, the combined vote of Taft and Roosevelt exceeding his. But Wilson won by an electoral majority that was a record at the time. In the popular voting on November 5, 1912, Wilson received 6,293,454 votes, Roosevelt 4,119,538, and Taft 3,484,980. Wilson won the Presidency with 435 electoral votes from forty states. Roosevelt received 88 votes from six states and Taft eight from two. Eugene V. Debs polled 900,672 votes for the Socialists. Eugene W. Chafin of the Prohibition Party received 206,275. Arthur E. Reimer of Massachusetts, Socialist Labor candidate, received 28,750.

Wilson's rapid rise to the Presidency was considered a political phenomenon. Until he was elected governor of New Jersey, he had never been a political candidate. From the time Wilson took his first public office in 1911 until he was elected to the nation's highest, only one year and 303 days elapsed. Wilson was not offered to the Democratic national convention as a "dark horse," however. He already had attracted national attention during the short time he was New Jersey governor. He exercised his executive powers to force the state's Democratic "bosses" to bow to his administration.

New Jersey, long known as an indulgent state toward big business and monopolies, was given new and stringent control laws. Such reforms as employers' liability for workers' accidents were instituted. The platform on which Wilson was elected governor was fulfilled to the last plank. Colonel Edward M. House of Texas, Wilson's personal advisor, saw to it that these New Jersey accomplishments were exploited. Wilson was president of Princeton University when offered the nomination for governor. Until then, he had been known chiefly as a college professor and writer.

Woodrow Wilson was born at Staunton, Virginia, on December 28, 1856—the eighth President born in that state. He was the son of a prominent Presbyterian minister. His family moved successively to Augusta, Georgia, and Columbia, South Carolina. Wilson attended Davidson College, Princeton, and the University of Virginia Law School. After his admission to the bar to practice law, he received a doctor's degree in political science from Johns Hopkins University.

1913

PARCEL POST SERVICE went into effect on January 1, 1913—to the particular delight of the rural districts. Parcel post was one of several improvements in the postal and communications fields which Taft sponsored. The Parcel Post Act was passed by Congress in August, 1912, providing for the delivery of packages of moderate weight and size at reasonable rates. Previously, intercity deliveries of packages on a commercial basis had been handled by private companies. Complaints of high charges and poor service constantly reached the government.

Farmers of America were gratified by the introduction of the parcel post. The catalogue mail order business was increasing in volume and parcel post was the answer to an irritating delivery problem. During the first week of the new service's operation, an estimated 6,000,000 packages were sent by parcel post. Another expansion of post office services was the establishment of the postal savings bank system. Through a law passed in 1910, many post offices became convenient savings banks. Deposits were accepted and guaranteed safe keeping, with the depositors receiving two per cent interest on their savings.

The Mann-Elkins Act of 1910 placed communications under supervision of the Interstate Commerce Commission. This included telephone, telegraph, cable and wireless. A new and exciting type of communications was developing—radio entertainment. The first broadcast of a musical composition was made by Lee De Forest from Telharmonic Hall in New York to the Brooklyn Navy Yard. Pioneer radio amateurs who picked it up heard Rossini's *William Tell Overture*.

Parcel post service was hailed by farmers. Their mail order goods were guaranteed speedy delivery.

An estimated 6,000,000 packages were delivered the first week. Postal savings banks were another service introduced by the Post Office.

781

1913

A TALKING MOTION PICTURE! Thomas Edison demonstrated in his laboratory at Orange, New Jersey, a picture which not only moved but "talked!" The demonstration on January 3, 1913, marked another step in the rapid advancement of motion pictures. Edison solved many of the early problems of the movies. In 1904, he developed the cameraphone, the first moving picture with sound. In 1909, he joined with Biograph and Vitagraph in forming the Motion Picture Patents Company. By then the "nickelodeon" (nickel movie) had been introduced by John P. Harris and Harry Davis of Pittsburgh. Nearly 10,000 of the little movie houses were operating in America and consolidated producing companies were needed to provide films. Famous Players Film Company (later Paramount) was organized in 1912. The motion picture "capital" had shifted from New York to Hollywood. Suspense film serials were popular and the motion picture market was expanding rapidly. Movie heroines of the day included Pearl White of *The Perils of Pauline* and Ruth Roland of *Ruth of the Rockies*. Edwin S. Porter, who produced *The Great Train Robbery* in 1903, was recognized as the "father of the story film." The earliest motion picture subjects had been confined to such news events and celebrations as parades, sports contests, and public ceremonies.

1913

A PERMANENT INCOME TAX on individual and corporate earnings was added to the Constitution. The Sixteenth Amendment, legalizing the tax, was declared ratified and in effect on February 25, 1913. The amendment provided: "The Congress shall have power to lay and collect taxes on incomes, from whatever source derived, without apportionment among the several states, and without regard to any census or enumeration." A long-standing issue was settled—Americans would pay an income tax.

The income tax was not new in the United States. During the Civil War, the Union had levied a tax on earnings to help defray expenses of the conflict. The act, passed in 1861, provided for a three per cent levy on income in excess of $800 per year. Later the rate was increased to five per cent on incomes between $600 and $5,000, with a ten per cent tax on all higher earnings. The constitutionality of income taxes was not questioned at the time, as the North willingly paid the government's revenues needed to carry on the fight.

During Cleveland's administration, an attempt was made to establish a permanent income tax. The act, passed in 1894, specified a tax of two per cent on incomes above $4,000. The next year, the Supreme Court declared the income tax law unconstitutional because it was not based on population. When an income tax law was proposed again during Taft's term, it was apparent that a constitutional change was necessary. The Sixteenth Amendment was the outcome and it placed no limit on the amount of the tax. What the rate of the income tax would be was left to Congress' discretion.

1913

EXISTENCE OF A "MONEY TRUST," gripping America's finances, long had been suspected. The House authorized its committee on banking and currency to make an investigation. A subcommittee headed by Arsene P. Pujo of Louisiana began hearings in April, 1912. In its report on February 28, 1913, the Pujo committee asserted that there was "a great and rapidly growing concentration of control of money and credit in the hands of a few men." The nation was shocked and angered by these Pujo accusations.

The Pujo committee's hearings often were stormy. Many prominent bankers and financiers testified. Among them was J. Pierpont Morgan, the New York banker. Piercing of eye and caustic in comment, Morgan was not disconcerted by the pointed questions asked him. Sometimes he pounded the table. Once, when asked if he had a competitive advantage over other banks, he replied, "I do not compete for any deposits. I do not care whether they come. They come." Morgan asserted before the committee members that all of the banks in the world "could not control money." There could be no "money trust," he said.

Other witnesses gave sufficient testimony to convince the Pujo committee that a "money trust" not only was possible, but very likely. In its report, the committee said that the nation's credit and money control were concentrated in Wall Street. They attributed the "money trust" to a combination of several banks, trust companies and insurance firms. The control was held through purchase of stock in a wide range of smaller companies and interlocking of directorships. The domination was described as extending over industry, railroads, public utilities and financial firms. The Pujo committee made its report four days before the inauguration of President Woodrow Wilson, who regarded trusts and monopolies as nothing short of economic evil.

1913

A SEPARATE LABOR DEPARTMENT was created by Congress on March 4, 1913—the day that Wilson was inaugurated. A single Department of Commerce and Labor had been established in 1903 and now Congress separated the two divisions. Each became a full-fledged department with cabinet status. On his first day in office, Wilson appointed the two new Secretaries. William B. Wilson of Pennsylvania was named Secretary of Labor and William C. Redfield of New York became Secretary of Commerce. The new Labor Secretary was sponsored by the American Federation of Labor.

From the start, Wilson demonstrated his determination to be an individualistic President. Wilson once had said, "The President is at liberty, both in law and conscience, to be as big a man as he can. His capacity will set the limit." Wilson in his inaugural address declared that free enterprise must be upheld. He said that not only must the natural resources of the land be conserved, but also the human resources of its people. Wilson's over-all policy was known as the "New Freedom." He demanded reforms in the banking system and business regulations. The President advocated a new labor policy and encouraged conservation and agriculture. He asked for lower tariffs.

Ten days after entering office, Wilson won favor with the newspapermen. He held a press conference which was open to all reporters covering the White House. In the past, conferences had been open only to an invited few. Wilson broke another custom on April 8. He appeared before a special session of Congress to deliver personally a message on tariff revision. The last President to appear in person on such occasions was John Adams in 1800. All Presidents since then had sent their messages to the Capitol, to be read by congressional clerks.

☆ 785 ☆

1913

CHINA BECAME A REPUBLIC when the ruling Manchu dynasty was overthrown. The father of the Chinese revolution (1911-1912) was Dr. Sun Yat-sen. Dr. Sun backed three principles: nationalism, democracy and livelihood. When the revolution broke out he was in the United States collecting funds from overseas Chinese to help create a new government. He returned to China and was made president, but soon stepped aside in favor of another leader, Yuan Shih-kai, in order to preserve unity. When Yuan later tried to restore the monarchy Sun again became president.

Recognition of China's new government by the United States came on May 2, 1913. America was one of the first nations to do this. The tradition of friendship with China was of long standing. The United States had not taken the same aggressive action as other nations in obtaining trading privileges. The Open Door policy had been fostered to maintain equal opportunity in the Far East. After the Boxer Rebellion the United States remitted part of the payment made by the Chinese for use of Chinese students sent to study in American colleges and universities. Upon returning, these students were better able to help their young Chinese republic.

America's bankers had been discouraged from investing in a Chinese loan a few weeks prior to the recognition, but not because of lack of friendship. China requested a loan of $125,000,000. The bankers turned to Washington for encouragement, but Wilson refused to offer it. The President said that the sovereignty of China was involved and the loan might lead to intervention by some other foreign power. American private investors could expect no help from their government, he warned. The bankers called off the negotiations and small businessmen in the United States cheered the so-called "rebuff of Wall Street."

William Jennings Bryan, who was named Secretary of State by Wilson, figured in other important foreign relations at the time. Bryan devised a plan for "cooling off" treaties, whereby each signer would agree to refer disputes to a commission. All military action was prohibited until the commission gave a decision, with a time limit of one year. Thirty such treaties were finally signed.

1913

DIRECT ELECTION OF SENATORS by the people was adopted as a political reform. The Seventeenth Amendment, ratified on May 31, 1913, provided for United States senators to be chosen by popular vote. Since the beginning of American constitutional government, the senators had been elected only by the state legislatures. The system long had been regarded as an open invitation to bribery and corruption by those men desirous of achieving senatorial seats. Wealthy men who wanted to attain the prestige of senatorships frequently were accused of buying their seats. Corporations of many kinds, wanting their own men in the Senate, found they had only to exert the proper amount of influence.

Four times since 1894 the House of Representatives supported amendments to change the system. Each time the Senate blocked the measure. Finally, in a voter rebellion, the people forced the reform. Nevada in 1899 adopted a system requiring its legislators to support senatorial candidates selected in primary elections. By 1912, thirty states had similar laws. This not only demonstrated the will of the people, it sent senators to Washington willing to vote for the amendment.

The direct primary election was one of a number of political reforms effected in many states. The initiative system gave voters the right to propose laws. The referendum put to popular vote, for approval or rejection, laws passed by the legislatures. Recall laws, adopted in some states, gave the public the right to vote out of office an elected official considered derelict in his duty. Political domination steadily was being taken from the "bosses" and put in the hands of the voters.

1913

THE TARIFFS WERE LOWERED as one of Wilson's first steps to carry out his program. On October 3, 1913, the President signed the Underwood-Simmons Tariff Act. It represented the first effective move to reduce the protective tariffs since the Civil War. The new duties were lowered to an average of approximately thirty per cent, compared to the forty per cent average of the Payne-Aldrich tariffs. The rates were reduced on several hundred products, wool, iron, steel and later sugar being put on the free list (no duty charged). Some protective features were retained in the new tariff schedules.

Wilson believed, along with most of the Democrats, that a high protective tariff was the "mother of trusts." He considered high tariffs as special benefits to big business and manufacturing monopolies. The pro-tariff forces, opposing the Underwood-Simmons Act, maintained that the curbs on more cheaply manufactured foreign goods protected the jobs and wages of American workers. Senator Oscar Underwood of Alabama, in preparing the new tariff schedule, received strong support from the President. Manufacturers sent lobbyists to Washington to seek support in maintaining a high tariff. Wilson publicly denounced those who were lobbying for special interests and prevented any serious changes in the proposed tariff. The lobbyists retreated.

Income tax rates were established and put into effect to offset the loss of tariff revenues. The schedule levied a one per cent tax against incomes between $3,000 and $20,000, with a $4,000 minimum for married couples. The tax rates were scaled upward with a maximum of six per cent on $500,000 or more.

FEDERAL RESERVE BANKS were created by Congress in answer to Wilson's plea for financial reform. The President sought to lessen control over money and credit held by a few bankers. The Glass-Owen Act of December 23, 1913, drafted by Senator Carter Glass of Virginia, provided for federal reserve banks in twelve national districts. The reserve banks did no public business, serving only banks. All national banks were required to join the Federal Reserve System and state banks were given the option. Each member bank subscribed six per cent of its capital to federal reserve capital stock. The federal reserve units could issue banknotes based on their collateral and gold reserve. The reserve banks could make loans to members to avert a crisis. The reserve banks also served as depositories for national banks' cash reserves. The Federal Reserve System was put under the direction of a board of seven members. The Federal Reserve was the fifth national banking system to be adopted by the government. Banks of the United States were chartered in 1791 and 1816. An independent treasury system, adopted in 1840, provided for the federal funds to be deposited in vaults or sub-treasuries. The National Banking Act of 1863 made it a requirement that banks with national charters subscribe one-third of their capital to the United States government securities.

Mexico Overthrew Diaz, Dictator For 33 Years—

Porfirio Diaz, after ruling as dictator for thirty-three years, was overthrown in 1910 by a revolution in Mexico. A period of conflict followed, ultimately leading to intervention by the United States. About 50,000 Americans lived in Mexico and United States investments in the nation totaled a billion dollars.

Francisco Madero led the rebellion which drove Diaz into exile. Madero attempted to establish a democracy and President Taft recognized his administration. The Mexican government was in good financial condition, but the nation's 15,000,000 people were impoverished and unhappy.

Madero was captured and murdered during another insurrection. The hand of suspicion was pointed at Victoriano Huerta, the new rebel chief. President Wilson refused to recognize Huerta, whom he called a tyrant. Wilson would not "force Huerta on the poor people."

—United States Marines Occupied Vera Cruz

Wilson induced twenty-six other nations, including Great Britain, to withdraw recognition of Huerta. The United States fleet blockaded Vera Cruz to prevent shipment of arms to Huerta. Arms sent to Venustiano Carranza and "Pancho" Villa were permitted to pass, however.

A clash between American and Mexican forces finally came on April 9, 1914. American sailors loading supplies at Tampico were arrested. Although the Americans were freed with an apology, the dispute with Huerta mounted and Wilson ordered fourteen battleships to Vera Cruz. United States Marines occupied the city on April 21. Nineteen Americans were killed in the fight. War with Mexico appeared imminent.

Wilson accepted an offer of mediation by Argentina, Brazil and Chile. But Huerta fled to Spain and a provisional government was established under Carranza. Political and agricultural reforms were promised by Carranza. Although withholding recognition at the time, Wilson waived indemnity and the Marines were withdrawn in November.

1914

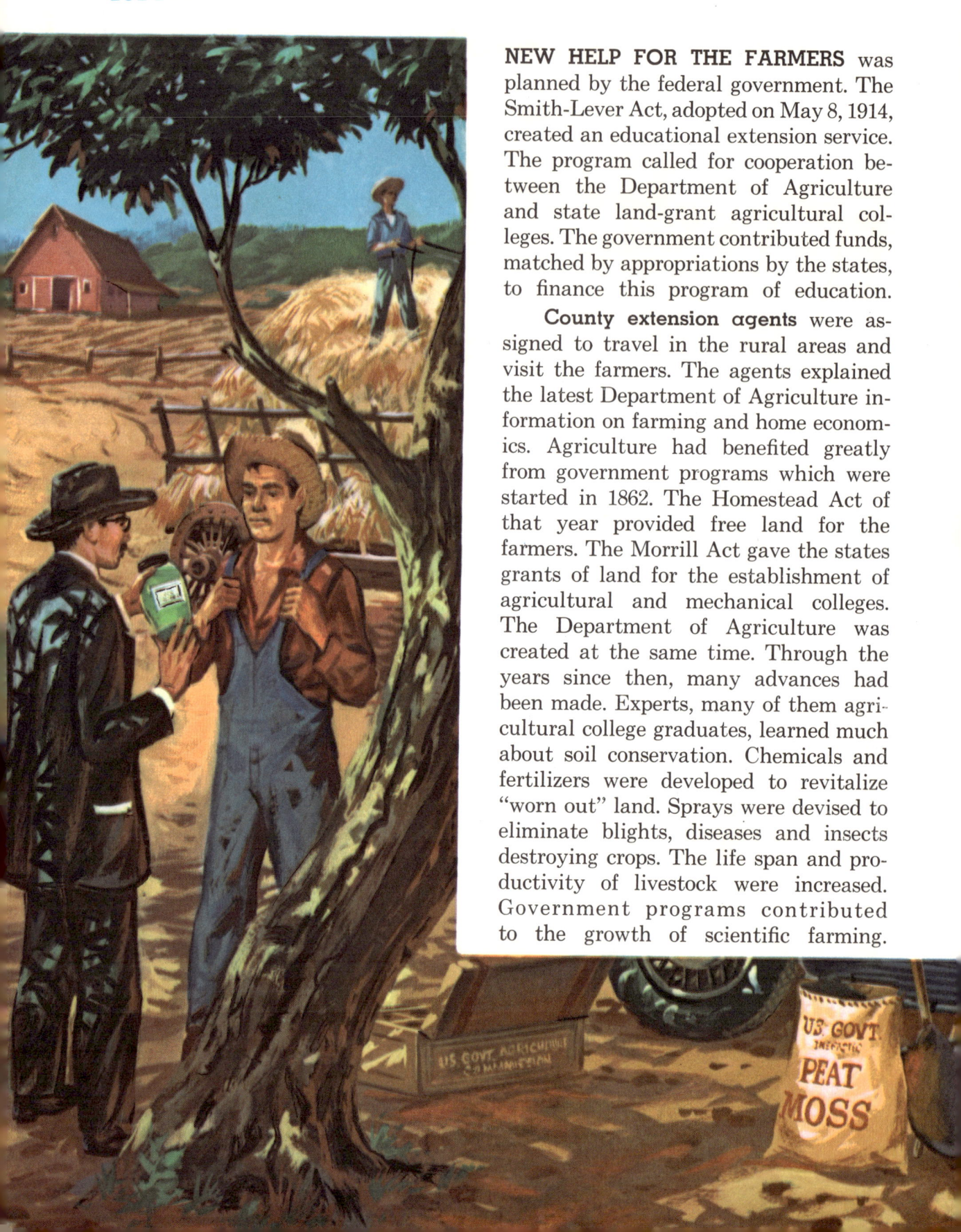

NEW HELP FOR THE FARMERS was planned by the federal government. The Smith-Lever Act, adopted on May 8, 1914, created an educational extension service. The program called for cooperation between the Department of Agriculture and state land-grant agricultural colleges. The government contributed funds, matched by appropriations by the states, to finance this program of education.

County extension agents were assigned to travel in the rural areas and visit the farmers. The agents explained the latest Department of Agriculture information on farming and home economics. Agriculture had benefited greatly from government programs which were started in 1862. The Homestead Act of that year provided free land for the farmers. The Morrill Act gave the states grants of land for the establishment of agricultural and mechanical colleges. The Department of Agriculture was created at the same time. Through the years since then, many advances had been made. Experts, many of them agricultural college graduates, learned much about soil conservation. Chemicals and fertilizers were developed to revitalize "worn out" land. Sprays were devised to eliminate blights, diseases and insects destroying crops. The life span and productivity of livestock were increased. Government programs contributed to the growth of scientific farming.

WAR EXPLODED IN EUROPE and the United States proclaimed its neutrality! The long smoldering enmities burst into conflict and involved all of Europe's major powers. The stunning chain of events began with a Serbian patriot's assassination of Archduke Franz Ferdinand, heir to the Austrian throne, in Bosnia. Austria declared war on Serbia on July 28, 1914. Russia mobilized to aid Serbia and, on August 1, Germany declared war on Russia. Two days later, Germany declared war on France, Russia's ally, and invaded Belgium. On August 4, England rushed to Belgium's aid and declared war on Germany. Opposing forces were set.

The individual war moves immediately merged into a general conflict between the Allied and Central Powers. On August 4-5, President Wilson declared America's neutrality toward all. Wilson's neutrality proclamations were based on American tradition. In 1793, George Washington declared America's neutrality in regard to a war between England and France. In 1794, Congress passed a Neutrality Act forbidding United States citizens to enlist in the forces of a warring foreign nation. The outfitting in America of belligerent warships was prohibited by this act. After proclaiming neutrality, Wilson offered to mediate the European war under the Hague peace convention.

Kaiser Wilhelm sent a note to Wilson defending Germany's war declarations and invasion of Belgium. The President in a message to the nation asked Americans to "be neutral in fact as well as name ... impartial in thought as well as action." Secretary of State Bryan asked American banks not to lend money to any belligerent, as it would violate neutrality.

1914

THE PANAMA CANAL WAS OPENED to traffic and the first ocean steamship passed through on August 15, 1914. Seven years had elapsed since Colonel George W. Goethals was appointed chief engineer and began actual construction in April, 1907. The cost of building the canal was $275,000,000 and the United States spent an additional $113,000,000 on its fortification. The canal provided a water passage across the Isthmus of Panama from the Caribbean Sea to the Pacific Ocean. From deep water to deep water, a fifty-mile route was carved out in what was acclaimed as a marvel of engineering.

A lock-and-lake system enabled the largest ships to traverse the canal, avoiding the long voyage around South America. A dam was built near the mouth of the Chagres River on the Caribbean side, creating an inland Gatun Lake at an elevation of eighty-five feet. Locks at each terminus of the canal raised entering ships to the level of the lake. The same locks lowered the ships to sea level as they exited from Lake Gatun. The ships were drawn through the locks by locomotives operating on tracks laid alongside the waterways of the canal.

A diplomatic dispute with England arose over Panama Canal tolls. The Hay-Pauncefote Treaty of 1901, in which Great Britain surrendered isthmian canal rights, guaranteed that all nations would pay equal canal tolls. In 1912, Congress exempted American coastwise shipping from paying the tolls. England protested this act as contrary to the terms of the Hay-Pauncefote treaty. President Wilson, after a bitter fight with Congress, had the exemption repealed. In return, the leaders of Great Britain accepted the United States policy in regard to the Huerta government in Mexico.

A BLOW AT THE TRUSTS was struck by Wilson as he carried out a third step in his "New Freedom" platform. On September 26, 1914, the Federal Trade Commission Act was adopted. The measure was aimed at corporations and monopolies employing unfair methods of competition. The Trade Commission was created and given the power to issue "cease and desist" orders against offending companies or corporations. The "stop" orders were subject to review by the federal courts. The Federal Trade Commission was set up as bi-partisan and consisted of five members. It replaced the former Bureau of Corporations, whose function was to investigate and report on corporations under suspicion of restraint of trade.

The Federal Trade Commission was given police powers. It was authorized to demand annual or special reports from corporations and could conduct hearings. Congress gave the commission the authority to publish its findings, considering this an added weapon, as no corporations would relish the unfavorable publicity and criticism. The Trade Commission subsequently listed some of the methods which it considered to be unfair to competition. These included trade boycotts, mislabeling and adulteration of products, and false claims of patents to discourage manufacture by competitors.

Wilson's program made marked progress in eighteen months. The Underwood-Simmons Act carried out his plans to reduce protective tariffs—the Federal Reserve Act provided reform in national banking, currency control and credit. And now Wilson, with formation of the Federal Trade Commission, had struck at his bitterest foes—the monopolies.

Clayton Anti-Trust Act Strengthened Sherman Law

The Clayton Anti-Trust Act of October 15, 1914, broadened and strengthened the Sherman Anti-Trust Act. It defined violations.

The purchasing of stock in rival companies to lessen competition was prohibited. Interlocking directorates in business combinations with $1,000,000 capital were banned. Interlocking directorates had the same men on more than one board.

The officers and directors of corporations or combinations violating the Clayton Act were held individually responsible for the offenses.

Price-fixing and monopolies, to put competitors out of business, were declared illegal. Tying contracts, which required the dealer to use seller's products exclusively, were forbidden by Clayton Act.

Labor unions and agricultural organizations were exempted from anti-trust provisions. Strikes, peaceful picketing and boycotts were permitted under the measure.

INDEX TO VOLUME 10

A

ABC powers: mediate Mexican trouble, 790-791
Aguinaldo, Emilio: Filipino leader, 743
Alaska: boundary dispute in Panhandle, 747
Aldrich, Nelson W.: writes high tariff act, 771
Algeciras, Spain: conference of powers, 756
Amendments: Fourteenth, 753; Sixteenth, 783; Seventeenth, 787
Anti-Saloon League: 731
Anti-trust legislation: 746, 796
Argentina: in Venezuelan debt question, 745
Arizona: admitted as state, 777

B

Ballinger, Richard A.: Secretary of Interior in conservation dispute, 772-773
Beard, Daniel C.: in Boy Scout movement, 774
"Big Stick" diplomacy: in Alaskan boundary dispute, 747
Boy Scouts of America: 774
Bryan, William Jennings: in election of 1908, 766; as Wilson's Secretary of State, 786; favors neutrality, 793
Bunau-Varilla, Philippe: encourages revolt in Panama, 748

C

Canada: Klondike boundary dispute, 747
Cannon, Joseph G.: power as Speaker reduced, 771
Carnegie, Andrew: steel magnate in philanthropic causes, 737
Carranza, Venustiano: Mexican leader, 790-791
Castro, Cipriano: Venezuelan dictator in debt crisis, 744
China: becomes republic and is recognized by United States, 786
Clayton Anti-Trust Act: 796
Clayton-Bulwer Treaty: abrogated, 736
Colombia: in Panama Canal negotiations, 742, 748
Commerce, Department of: separate cabinet office created, 785
Commerce and Labor, Department of: created, 746
Conservation: Newlands Reclamation and Forest Reserve Acts, 741; 1908 conference spurs movement, 765; controversy in Taft administration, 772-773
Cuba: government of, 733; evacuated by American troops, 738
Czolgosz, Leon: assassinates President McKinley, 734

D

Danbury Hatters Case: Supreme Court rules against labor union, 763
De Forest, Lee: radio pioneer, 781
Diaz, Porfirio: Mexican dictator, 790
Dominican Republic: see Santo Domingo
Drago Doctrine: 745; revised, 762
Drago, Luis: protests against forceable collection of debts, 745

E

Edison, Thomas A.: develops sound films, 782
Elections: of 1904, 751; of 1908, 766; of 1912, 780
Elkins Act: forbids railroad rebates, 746
Entente Cordiale: 756

F

Federal Reserve System: established by Glass-Owen Act, 789
Federal Trade Commission: created, 795
Foraker Act: 732
Ford, Henry: mass produces autos, 769
Forest Reserve Act: 741
Fourteenth Amendment: applied to labor laws, 753
France: joins England in Entente Cordiale, 756
French Panama Canal Company: negotiates to sell canal rights, 742, 748

G

"Gentlemen's Agreement": limits Japanese immigration, 764
Germany: in Venezuelan debts question, 744, 745
Glass-Owen Act: creates Federal Reserve System, 789
Glavis, Louis R.: in conservation dispute, 772
Goethals, Colonel George W.: appointed chief engineer in construction of Panama Canal, 760
Gorgas, Major William C.: fights yellow fever in Cuba, 730; in Panama, 760
Gospel of Wealth: reveals Carnegie's philosophy, 737
Great Britain: in Venezuelan debt question, 744, 745; in Alaskan boundary dispute, 747; joins France in Entente Cordiale, 756

H

Havana, Cuba: in yellow fever campaign, 730
Hay-Bunau-Varilla Treaty: grants United States rights in Panama, 748
Hay, John: in Roosevelt cabinet, 735; in Panama canal developments, 742, 748
Hay-Pauncefote Treaty: gives United States right to construct isthmian canal, 736
Holmes, Oliver Wendell: Supreme Court Justice in Lochner vs. New York, 753
Honduras: and "dollar diplomacy," 776
House, Colonel Edward M.: advises Wilson, 780
Huerta, Victoriano: establishes Mexican government, 790-791

I

Income tax: legalized by Sixteenth Amendment, 783; rates established, 788
Insular cases: Supreme Court rules on status of possessions, 732
Interstate Commerce Act: powers limited by court action, 746

J

Japan: in war with Russia, 755; and immigration to America, 764

K

Kansas: and temperance movement, 731
Knox, Philander C.: as Attorney General, 750; Secretary of State, 776

L

Labor, Department of: separate cabinet office created, 785
La Follette, Robert M.: Republican Progressive, 771
Lochner vs. New York: Supreme Court rules on labor laws, 753
Lusitania: luxury liner makes first voyage, 761

M

Madero, Francisco: Mexican leader 790-791
Mann-Elkins Act: 781
McKinley, William: assassinated, 734
Mexico: and relations with the United States, 790-791
Mitchell, John: mine workers' leader acts in Pennsylvania strike, 740
Monroe Doctrine: in Venezuelan debt question, 745; modified by Roosevelt Corollary, 752
Morgan, J. Pierpont: testifies before committee on money trusts, 784
Morocco: 756
"Muckrakers": reform writers, 757; attack Taft's tariff policy, 771; in conservation dispute, 772

N

Nation, Carry: crusades for temperance, 731
Neutrality: as policy of United States, 793
Newlands Reclamation Act: provides funds for irrigating dry land, 741
New Mexico: admitted as state, 777
Nicaragua: and Taft's "dollar diplomacy," 776
Northern Securities Company Case: Supreme Court Ruling against railroad trust, 750

P

Panama Canal: background of United States' involvement, 736; Spooner Act appropriates funds, 742; construction of, 760; opened, 794
Panama, Republic of: established after revolt against Colombia, 748
Parcel post: becomes part of postal service, 781
Parker, Alton B.: loses in election of 1904, 751
Payne-Aldrich Tariff: 771, 788
Peary, Robert E.: reaches North Pole, 770
Philippine Islands: Organic Act creates government, 743
Pinchot, Gifford: named chairman of conservation commission, 765; in conservation dispute, 772-773
Platt Amendment: limits Cuban independence, 733, 738
Port Arthur, Manchuria: Russian fleet defeated by Japan, 755
Portsmouth, New Hampshire: treaty signed ending Russo-Japanese War, 755
Postal savings banks: 781
Puerto Rico: government of, 732
Pujo, Arsene P.: heads House committee investigating money trust, 784
Pure Food and Drug Act: 759

R

Reed, Walter: 730
Rhodes, Cecil: background and philanthropies, 739
Roosevelt Corollary: 752, 754
Roosevelt, Theodore: inaugurated as President, 735; acts in coal strike, 740; encourages conservation, 741; in Venezuelan debt controversy, 744, 745; acts against trusts, 746, 750; "big stick" diplomacy, 747; elected in 1904, 751; announces Corollary to Monroe Doctrine, 752; mediates Russo-Japanese War and receives Nobel Peace Prize, 755; and Algeciras conference, 756; and "muckrakers," 757; asks for international court, 762; concludes "Gentlemen's Agreement" with Japan, 764; calls conservation conference, 765; orders fleet around the world, 768; encourages Boy Scout movement, 774; questions Taft's policies, 775; nominated by Progressives, 779; loses in election of 1912, 780

Root, Elihu: 733, 735
Root-Takahira Agreement: outlines common policy in Far East between Japan and the United States, 767
Russia: in war with Japan, 755; czar calls Second Hague Conference, 762
Russo-Japanese War: 755

S

San Francisco, California: in disastrous earthquake of 1906, 758
Santo Domingo (Dominican Republic): debt question evokes Roosevelt Corollary, 752; and United States intervention, 754
Second Hague International Conference: 762
Seventeenth Amendment: provides for direct election of senators, 787
Sherman Anti-Trust Act: cited in Northern Securities Company case, 750
Sixteenth Amendment: legalizes federal income tax, 783
Smith, Captain Edward J.: in sinking of Titanic, 778
Smith-Lever Act: creates educational extension service for farmers, 792
"Square Deal": program of Theodore Roosevelt, 740
Sun Yat-sen: Chinese statesman in new republic, 786
Supreme Court: rules in Insular cases, 732; in Northern Securities Company case, 750; interprets Fourteenth Amendment in Lochner vs. New York, 753; in Danbury Hatters case, 763

T

Taft Administration in Conservation Dispute: 772-773
Taft Commission: helps govern Philippine Islands, 743
Taft-Katsura Memorandum: United States and Japan recognize spheres of interest, 755
Taft, William Howard: governor-general of Philippine Islands, 735, 743; elected President, 766; and tariff question, 771; in conservation dispute, 772-773; and "dollar diplomacy," 776; renominated, 779; loses in election of 1912, 780
Titanic: sinking of, 778
Twentieth Century Opens: 728-729

U

Underwood-Simmons Tariff Act: lowers duties, 788
United Mine Workers: in coal strike of 1902, 740
United States and Mexican Troubles: 790-791

V

Venezuela: involvement with European nations over debt payments, 744
Vera Cruz, Mexico: occupied by United States Marines, 791

W

Wilhelm II: German emperor, 744, 745, 756, 793
Wilson, Woodrow: nominated by Democrats, 779; elected President, 780; outlines Presidential policy, 785; tariff program, 788; declares American neutrality in World War I, 793; and Mexico, 790-791; moves against trusts, 795
World War I: begins in Europe, 793
Wright Brothers: and first successful airplane, 749

Y

Yellow Fever: 730, 760